The Gift of Time: Tithing Your Day to God

A 40-Day Devotional Journey to Draw Close to God

A. Mark Gray Jr.

Copyright © 2024 A. Mark Gray Jr.

All rights reserved.

ISBN: 9798301032837

CONTENTS

	Acknowledgments	i
	Introduction: The Gift of Time	1
Day 1:	Begin with Presence	Pg 5
Day 2:	Trust and Surrender	Pg 8
Day 3:	Practicing Gratitude Out Loud	Pg 11
Day 4:	Trusting in God's Provision	Pg 14
Day 5:	Seeking God's Guidance	Pg 17
Day 6:	Strengthening Your Faith	Pg 20
Day 7:	Serving God by Serving Others	Pg 23
Day 8:	Embracing Humanity	Pg 26
Day 9:	Bearing Fruit in Keeping with Repentance	Pg 29
Day 10:	Celebrating Transformation and Renewal	Pg 32
Day 11:	Preserving in Faithfulness	Pg 35
Day 12:	Renewing Your Commitment	Pg 38
Day 13:	Surrendering Control	Pg 41
Day 14:	Cultivating Peace Through Trust	Pg 44
Day 15:	Celebrating Progress with	Pg 47
Day 16:	Protecting Sacred Time with God	Pg 50
Day 17:	Cultivating Gratitude as a Pathway to Joy	Pg 53
Day 18:	Embracing Forgiveness	Pg 56
Day 19:	Embracing God's Healing	Pg 59
Day 20:	Faithfulness in Small Steps	Pg 62

Day 21:	Renewing Your Perspective	Pg 65
Day 22:	Serving Others with Humility	Pg 68
Day 23:	Stepping Out of Your Comfort Zone to Serve Jesus	Pg 71
Day 24:	Embracing Faith with Childlike Trust	Pg 74
Day 25:	Building a Strong Foundation in God's Word	Pg 77
Day 26:	Embracing God's Peace	Pg 80
Day 27:	Trusting in God's Timing	Pg 83
Day 28:	Living with Purpose	Pg 86
Day 29:	Cultivating a Spirit of Generosity	Pg 89
Day 30:	Finding Strength in God During Challenges	Pg 92
Day 31:	Serving Others in New Ways	Pg 95
Day 32:	Seeking God's Wisdom in Decisions	Pg 98
Day 33:	The Power of Supplication and Praying for Others	Pg 101
Day 34:	Cultivating a Heart of Gratitude	Pg 104
Day 35:	The Importance of Studying God's Word	Pg 107
Day 36:	Developing a Heart of Humility	Pg 110
Day 37:	Walking in the Spirit	Pg 113
Day 38:	Bearing Fruit in Every Season	Pg 116
Day 39:	Strengthened in Weakness	Pg 119
Day 40:	A Heart of Worship	Pg 122
	Closing Reflection: A Journey of Intentional Giving and Closeness to God	Pg 125

ACKNOWLEDGMENTS

First and foremost, I want to acknowledge the Holy Spirit for guiding me on my spiritual journey and inspiring every word of this devotional. Without His presence, none of this would have been possible.

To my beloved wife, Paula, my best friend and constant source of encouragement—thank you for your unwavering love and support. You are my partner in faith and life, and I'm forever grateful for you.

I extend my deepest gratitude to my pastor, Elvin Butts, and his wife, Paula, for their leadership, wisdom, and prayers that have shaped my walk with God. Your example has been a blessing in my life.

To my mother and father, thank you for your unceasing prayers and love, which brought me back to Jesus. You never gave up on me, and for that, I am eternally grateful.

To my twin brother, Jarvis, thank you for inspiring me to do more and for our wonderful conversations about the Lord. Your faith and encouragement push me to be better every day.

Finally, I give all glory to my Lord and Savior, Jesus Christ, for bringing this lost sheep back into His fold. Thank you for Your mercy, grace, and the everlasting love that saved me.

This devotional is a testament to the work God is doing in my life, and I pray it blesses others as much as I have been blessed in writing it.

INTRODUCTION: THE GIFT OF TIME

This book began as a personal journey. Like many, I always thought of tithing as something we did with money—an act of financial obedience to God. But I felt a gentle nudge over time, an invitation to go deeper. What if I could give back to God, not just from my wallet, but from my day, time, and talents? One day, while listening to a message about tithing, I began following along in my Bible. Many consider the first example of tithing to be when Abram (later known as Abraham) gave ten percent of his spoils to King Melchizedek. As it says in Genesis 14:18-20 (NKJV):

"Then Melchizedek, king of Salem, brought out bread and wine; he was the priest of God Most High. And he blessed him and said: 'Blessed be Abram of God Most High, Possessor of heaven and earth; And blessed be God Most High, Who has delivered your enemies into your hand.' And he gave him a tithe of all."

This passage reflects Abraham's response to God's provision. He gave Melchizedek a tenth of the spoils—not just gold or silver, but a portion of everything gained in that victory. It was not about material wealth alone but a humble acknowledgment of God's hand in his success.

One important point to remember is to support your local church and pastor. In the Old Testament, the Levites were set apart to serve in the temple, and the tithe was provided as their inheritance because they had no land of their own. *"The Levites have no portion or inheritance with Israel; they shall eat the offerings of the Lord made by fire, and His inheritance"* (Deuteronomy 18:1). Today, our pastors and churches rely on the generous support of their congregations. God loves a cheerful giver (2 Corinthians 9:7), and our giving should be a joyful act of worship.

In the same way, I realized that tithing is not only about what is in our wallets. It can be about offering our time, talents, and energy—recognizing God's work in every area of life. This devotional is an invitation to see what it means to give God the *first fruits* of our day, our hearts, and our lives. God promises in His Word that when we seek Him, we will find Him. *"Draw near to God, and He will draw near to you"* (James 4:8).

Whether you are a new believer or have been in your faith for decades, your relationship with God will continue to grow as you seek to know Him better. God loves you so much that He gave His only begotten Son for everyone (John 3:16). *"We love Him because He first loved us"* (1 John 4:19). Because He sought us first, it is essential to spend time nurturing our relationship with Him so that we may find and fulfill our life's purpose. Many of us ask, "What is my purpose in life?" It is a question that seems simple but is profound. When God looks at us, what does He see? Ultimately, it comes down to this: Does God see Jesus when He looks at you? This is something only you can answer. The purpose of this devotional is to help you spend time with our Lord and Savior, building a relationship that reflects His image more and more.

The Significance of 40 Days

So why a 40-day devotional, you might ask? In the Bible, 40 days hold great significance, representing times of testing, transformation, and preparation. Like many other numbers in Scripture, it has symbolic power, reminding us that God often uses these periods to draw people closer to Him and prepare them for His purposes.

Old Testament Examples
- **Noah's 40 Days and Nights of Rain**: During the flood, rain fell for 40 days and nights, and Noah and his family trusted God for deliverance (*Genesis 7:12*). This period was a test of faith and obedience, much like our own journeys with God, where trust is essential.
- **Moses' 40 Days on Mount Sinai**: Moses spent 40 days on Mount Sinai, communing with God and receiving the Ten Commandments (*Exodus 24:18*). This time with God was marked by intimacy, reminding us that setting aside intentional time with Him allows us to receive His guidance and wisdom.
- **Israel's 40 Years in the Wilderness**: The Israelites wandered in the wilderness for 40 years, a time God used to prepare and transform them before they entered the Promised Land (*Deuteronomy 8:2*). It was a season of growth and learning, just as this devotional can be a time of spiritual preparation.

New Testament Examples
- **Jesus' 40 Days in the Wilderness**: Before beginning His ministry, Jesus fasted and prayed for 40 days, enduring temptation and drawing strength from God (*Matthew 4:1-2*). This reminds us that dedicating time to God strengthens us, enabling us to overcome challenges and align with His will.
- **Jesus' 40 Days with the Disciples After His Resurrection**: After

His resurrection, Jesus spent 40 days with His disciples, teaching them and preparing them for the work they would do in His name (*Acts 1:3*). This was a period of transformation for the disciples as they deepened their understanding of their mission.

These examples show that God has often used 40 days for renewal, instruction, and transformation—both in the Old and New Testaments. *Romans 12:2* reminds us of the purpose behind these times: *"Do not be conformed to this world, but be transformed by the renewing of your mind."*

Each day should be purposeful. After all, we are not promised tomorrow. *"You do not know what will happen tomorrow. For what is your life? It is even a vapor that appears for a little time and then vanishes away"* (James 4:14). A vapor moves quickly, and time can escape us all. So, whether we live to be 100 or less, that time is fleeting compared to eternity. *"See then that you walk circumspectly, not as fools but as wise, redeeming the time because the days are evil"* (Ephesians 5:15-16). Paul describes us as ambassadors for Christ called to a purpose in this world.

So, each day of this devotional will provide an opportunity to set aside intentional time with God—through prayer, Scripture, reflection, or a specific act of service. My hope is that by dedicating time each day, you will feel His presence more deeply and experience growth, transformation, and a renewed sense of purpose.

Whether you are just beginning your faith journey or have walked with God for years, these 40 days invite you to a fresh encounter with Him. Approach each day with an open heart, ready to receive, and trust that God will meet you right where you are.

Prayer of Dedication

Dear Heavenly Father, I come to You with a softened heart and a desire to seek You. You are holy and mighty, and I long to walk with You more closely. Help me to know You more deeply and to be transformed so that when You look at me, You see Your Son, Jesus. I desire to be filled and overflowing with Your Spirit. Please guide my walk, protect me, and let me be a light to others in this dark world. I give You all the praise, Lord, for You are holy and great. Lead me over these next 40 days to draw closer to You. Amen.

Starting Your Journey: How to Use This Devotional

This devotional is designed to be a companion for your heart and mind as you draw closer to God each day. Here are some helpful steps to make this journey meaningful and consistent.

1. Begin with Your First Minutes
   - Set the Tone for Your Day: Aim to make this devotional the first thing you read each morning. Allow these moments with God to frame your day before checking messages, news, or emails.

Embracing this habit can help start your day with purpose and peace.
- Sacred Time: Give God your best by dedicating the first minutes of your day to Him. Find a quiet place, open your heart, and invite His presence to guide you.

2. Consider a Devotional Partner
- Share the Journey: My wife and I often discuss our reflections, deepening our connection with God and our relationship as a couple. If you are married, consider sharing your thoughts together. This practice can bring both spiritual and relational growth.
- Find a Friend or Partner: If you are not married, consider asking a friend or family member to join you on this journey. A devotional partner can offer encouragement and accountability, creating a meaningful bond as you grow together in faith.

3. Daily Routine and Reflection
- Set Aside 10–15 Minutes: Each day, read the devotional passage, take a few minutes to reflect, and write down any insights or prayers. Start with a simple prayer, inviting God's guidance as you read and reflect.
- Journal Your Journey: Each devotional includes space for personal reflections. These notes can become a record of your growth and a reminder of how God is working in your life.
- Be Consistent and Graceful: If you miss a day, do not worry—simply pick up where you left off. This is a journey of grace, with space to grow at your own pace.

4. Expect Transformation
- Look for God's Presence: Through these 40 days, anticipate growth and transformation. Let each day bring you closer to God, trusting He is at work in every step.
- A Connection with God: This time is not only about reading but about nurturing a relationship. Trust that as you give God your first minutes, He will meet you in every moment, drawing you into deeper faith and understanding.

May this devotional inspire and renew your heart as you journey closer to God each day. Let's begin with expectation and gratitude, knowing God is ready to walk this path with you. With this foundation, let's step forward into the first day of this 40-day journey, ready to draw closer to God and experience His presence in new ways.

DAY 1: BEGIN WITH PRESENCE

Scripture Reading:

"Be still, and know that I am God." —Psalm 46:10 (NKJV)

Reflection:

Today, we start with something essential and simple: **being present with God**. Life is filled with distractions, but God invites us to come as we are, setting aside time to be with Him. We often think of tithing as giving something tangible, but today, we are tithing our **presence**—our willingness to sit in God's presence and listen without the need to do anything.

Consider today as the first step in building a deeper relationship with God. As with any relationship, it starts by spending time together, allowing ourselves to grow familiar with His presence and love. God desires to know us deeply and wants us to know Him deeply in return. Take a few minutes to set aside your concerns and be still, tuning your heart and mind to focus on God alone.

Prayer:

Dear Lord, today I come to You, ready to be still in Your presence. Help me to quiet my heart and mind, setting aside distractions so I can hear Your voice. Teach me what it means to know You more deeply. Help me trust that You are here with me and that You love me unconditionally. Today, I give You the first fruits of my time. I want to know You more. In Jesus' name, Amen.

Action Step:

Spend five to ten minutes in quiet reflection. If this is new to you, don't worry about what to think or say. Sit quietly, breathe deeply, and focus on God's presence. You might want to repeat today's verse, *"Be still, and know that I am God."* Allow these words to settle in your heart.

Journaling Prompt:

As you end your time of quiet reflection, take a moment to write down anything on your heart and mind. It could be a concern, a question, or something you feel burdened by. As you sit quietly, listen for what God may want to say in response. If you sense He's speaking, write it down.

Remember, a good way to discern if what you hear is truly from God is to test it against His Word. God's words will always align with His character and Scripture, bringing peace, encouragement, or gentle correction but never condemnation. *"For God is not the author of confusion but of peace"* (1 Corinthians 14:33, NKJV).

God desires purity, peace, and growth for us. He may reveal things in your life that need changing—perhaps something you're watching, listening to, or speaking that doesn't align with His purity and goodness. Jesus said, *"What comes out of the mouth defiles a man"* (Matthew 15:11, NKJV), reminding us to guard what we allow into our hearts and minds.

Use this time to listen closely. Is there an area He's prompting you to grow or change? Write down anything He shows you and reflect on how it aligns with the character of God as revealed in the Bible.

Reflection on the Journey Ahead:

Today, you've set aside a small portion of your day for God. Over the next few days, you'll continue to build this practice by seeking His presence and listening. By the end of the first week, we'll start thinking about how this closeness with God can lead us to serve others in small ways or through larger commitments. For now, know that this time with God is the foundation of everything we'll explore in the days ahead.

Day 1 Takeaway:

Today, you practiced the gift of presence—simply being with God. Trust that He values this time with you and that every moment you spend with Him strengthens your relationship.

DAY 2: TRUST AND SURRENDER

Scripture Reading:

"Cast all your anxiety on Him because He cares for you." —1 Peter 5:7 (NIV)

Reflection:

Today, we are invited to bring our concerns and anxieties before God and to **trust** Him with our burdens. Surrender is essential in our walk with God. It's more than just releasing our worries—it's an act of faith, trusting that God is big enough to handle all that weighs on our hearts.

It is easy to hold on to stress, doubt, or control, but God calls us to cast our cares upon Him. He does not want us carrying these burdens alone; He desires to walk alongside us, comfort, guide, and strengthen us. *"Come to me, all you who are weary and burdened, and I will give you rest"* (Matthew 11:28, NIV). Today, let's practice surrendering those things that might prevent us from fully trusting God.

Prayer:

Dear Lord, today I bring You my burdens, fears, and concerns. Help me to lay these down at Your feet, trusting in Your love and Your promises. I know that You care for me deeply and that You are strong enough to carry what I cannot. Please give me peace as I release these burdens and strengthen my faith in You. In Jesus' name, Amen.

Action Step:

Write down a few things you're currently carrying—any fears, worries, or situations weighing on you. As you write, imagine placing each one in God's hands. Take a moment to visualize yourself releasing control and allowing Him to take over.

Journaling Prompt:

Reflect on the experience of writing down your burdens. Did it feel difficult to surrender control? Is there an area in your life where it is particularly hard to trust God? Write down anything you felt God may be saying to you as you released these worries.

When learning to hear God's voice, it is essential to test it with Scripture. God's voice is full of truth and peace and always aligns with His Word. *"For I know the plans I have for you… plans to prosper you and not to harm you, plans to give you hope and a future"* (Jeremiah 29:11, NIV). God's words will bring comfort and encouragement, not fear. If you feel led, note any Scriptures that came to mind as you prayed.

Reflection on the Journey Ahead:

As you set aside time with God each day, remember that surrender is a process. God desires to be your safe place, the One you turn to with everything in your heart. The more you practice surrender, the more you'll experience His peace and strength in your daily life.

Day 2 Takeaway:

Today, you took a step toward surrender. Trust that God cares deeply for you and wants to carry your burdens. He is faithful, and you can find peace in His presence.

DAY 3: PRACTICING GRATITUDE OUT LOUD

Scripture Reading:

"In everything give thanks; for this is the will of God in Christ Jesus for you." —1 Thessalonians 5:18 (NKJV)

Reflection:

Today, let us focus on cultivating a heart of gratitude, not only in our minds but with our words. While our thoughts are powerful, there is something uniquely transformative about **speaking** our gratitude out loud. God calls us to give thanks in all circumstances, knowing that gratitude is an act of faith—it reminds us of His goodness and shifts our focus from what we lack to what He has already done.

By speaking gratitude aloud, we create an atmosphere of praise that can uplift us and those around us. *"Enter into His gates with thanksgiving, And into His courts with praise. Be thankful to Him, and bless His name"* (Psalm 100:4, NKJV). Today, let us practice bringing our gratitude into the open, thanking God for His presence in every moment of our lives.

Prayer:

Dear Lord, thank You for all You have done in my life, even in ways I may not fully see or understand. Teach me to speak gratitude in all things, big and small, and help me to see my circumstances through Your eyes. Fill my heart with thanksgiving, and give me the courage to proclaim Your goodness out loud. In Jesus' name, Amen.

Action Step:

Take a moment to list five things you are grateful for, then **speak each one out loud**. They could be people, opportunities, answered prayers, or even lessons learned through challenges. As you say each one, let yourself feel the gratitude that comes with acknowledging these blessings. This small act can lift your spirit and affirm God's presence in your life.

Journaling Prompt:

Reflect on how it felt to speak your gratitude aloud. Did it shift your perspective or bring new peace? Write down any feelings, insights, or surprises that came as you gave voice to your thankfulness.

As you journal, listen for what God might want to say to you about His blessings and goodness. Sometimes, God uses moments of gratitude to remind us of His love. If you sense Him saying something specific, write it down. Remember, God's voice will always align with His character and bring encouragement, as James 1:17 reminds us: *"Every good gift and every perfect gift is from above, and comes down from the Father of lights, with whom there is no variation or shadow of turning."*

Reflection on the Journey Ahead:

Gratitude shapes our faith and renews our minds. By practicing spoken gratitude, we develop a habit of proclaiming God's goodness, both in our hearts and with our voices. As we continue this 40-day journey, let us approach each day with a thankful heart, trusting that God is already working in every circumstance.

Day 3 Takeaway:

Today, you practiced the gift of spoken gratitude, acknowledging God's blessings out loud. Continue to seek a thankful heart, trusting God's goodness is present in all things

DAY 4: TRUSTING IN GOD'S PROVISION

Scripture Reading:

"And my God shall supply all your need according to His riches in glory by Christ Jesus."
—Philippians 4:19 (NKJV)

Reflection:

Today, let's focus on trusting God as our Provider. As we grow in gratitude, it becomes easier to see that every blessing and provision in our lives is a gift from God. When we trust in God's provision, we are reminded that He cares deeply for us and knows exactly what we need.

Sometimes, our needs feel overwhelming, and we might be tempted to rely solely on ourselves. But God invites us to place our trust in Him. *"Therefore do not worry, saying, 'What shall we eat?' or 'What shall we drink?' or 'What shall we wear?' ... For your heavenly Father knows that you need all these things"* (Matthew 6:31-32, NKJV). Today, let us rest in the assurance that God is aware of every need we have and He is more than able to provide.

Prayer:

Dear Lord, thank You for being my Provider. Help me trust You with my needs, knowing that You are faithful and care for me. Teach me to rely on You completely, even in times of uncertainty. I surrender my worries to You, trusting that You will supply all I need according to Your perfect will. In Jesus' name, Amen.

Action Step:

Write down one or two things you are currently concerned about, whether physical, emotional, or spiritual needs. As you write, imagine placing these needs in God's hands, trusting He knows exactly what you need and will provide in His perfect timing.

Speak aloud: "Lord, I trust You to provide for my needs. I know You see me and care deeply about what I am going through. Thank You for being my Provider.

Journaling Prompt:

Reflect on any worries or needs you have been holding onto. How does it feel to release them to God, trusting His provision? Write down any insights or peace that comes as you surrender these concerns to Him.

Take a few minutes to listen. If God speaks to your heart, write it down. His voice brings reassurance, encouragement, and hope. Remember, God's voice will always align with His Word, as Philippians 4:6-7 says: *"Be anxious for nothing, but in everything by prayer and supplication, with thanksgiving, let your requests be made known to God; and the peace of God, which surpasses all understanding, will guard your hearts and minds through Christ Jesus."*

Reflection on the Journey Ahead:

Learning to trust God's provision is an ongoing journey, but each step of surrender deepens our faith. As you continue this 40-day journey, remember that God's heart is to provide for you. Every need, no matter how big or small, matters to Him.

Day 4 Takeaway:

Today, you practiced trusting God with your needs, believing He will provide. Remember that God knows you intimately and cares deeply about every detail of your life.

DAY 5: SEEKING GOD'S GUIDANCE

Scripture Reading:

"Trust in the Lord with all your heart, and lean not on your own understanding; in all your ways acknowledge Him, and He shall direct your paths." —Proverbs 3:5-6 (NKJV)

Reflection:

Today, let us focus on seeking God's guidance in our lives. God's Word assures us that He is willing and able to direct our paths when we trust in Him wholeheartedly. Life brings choices and challenges, and it can be tempting to rely on our understanding. Yet, God invites us to acknowledge Him in every area, promising to make our paths straight.

Seeking God's guidance requires humility and openness. It means setting aside our assumptions and asking Him to lead. *"Your ears shall hear a word behind you, saying, 'This is the way, walk in it,' whenever you turn to the right hand or whenever you turn to the left"* (Isaiah 30:21, NKJV). God's voice brings clarity and peace, directing us in ways that honor Him.

Prayer:

Dear Lord, thank You for being my Guide. Help me to seek Your wisdom above my understanding and to rely on You in every decision I make. Open my heart to Your voice, and lead me on the path that aligns with Your will. I surrender my plans to You, trusting You know what is best for me. In Jesus' name, Amen.

Action Step:

Think of an area in your life where you need guidance—perhaps a decision, a relationship, or a personal goal. Take a moment to ask God to lead you in this area, seeking His wisdom rather than relying solely on your understanding.

Speak aloud: "Lord, I invite You to guide me. Help me to follow Your direction, trusting that You know the best path for me. Thank You for being my faithful Guide."

Journaling Prompt:

Reflect on the area where you are seeking God's guidance. Write down any thoughts or ideas that come to mind as you seek His wisdom. Are there areas where you find it challenging to relinquish control or lean on God's direction?

Take time to listen for His voice, asking for peace and clarity. If you sense God speaking, write down what you hear. Remember, God's guidance often brings peace, patience, and understanding, as promised in Psalm 32:8: *"I will instruct you and teach you in the way you should go; I will guide you with My eye."* God's wisdom will always align with His Word and bring you closer to His heart.

Reflection on the Journey Ahead:

Each time we seek God's guidance, we strengthen our trust in Him. As we continue this 40-day journey, remember that God delights in directing our paths. He is a faithful Guide who leads us with wisdom, grace, and love.

Day 5 Takeaway:

Today, you practiced seeking God's guidance, inviting Him to direct your steps. Trust that His guidance will bring peace and clarity, helping you to walk confidently in His will.

DAY 6: STRENGTHENING YOUR FAITH

Scripture Reading:

"Now faith is the substance of things hoped for, the evidence of things not seen." — Hebrews 11:1 (NKJV)

Reflection:

Today, we are focusing on strengthening our faith in God's promises. Faith is trusting in what we cannot yet see, believing in God's Word even when our circumstances feel uncertain. True faith holds on to God's promises, finding assurance in His unfailing love and faithfulness.

Strengthening our faith means choosing to believe that God is working, even in the unseen. When we walk by faith, we are reminded of His great love and power, knowing that *"All things work together for good to those who love God, to those who are the called according to His purpose"* (Romans 8:28, NKJV). Today, let us reaffirm our faith, trusting in God's goodness and standing firm on His promises.

Prayer:

Dear Lord, thank You for being faithful and true to Your promises. Strengthen my faith today, helping me to trust You even when I cannot see the whole picture. Give me the confidence to walk by faith and not by sight, knowing that You are always with me. Help me to hold on to Your promises and to believe in Your goodness in every circumstance. In Jesus' name, Amen.

Action Step:

Identify an area in your life where you feel uncertain or are waiting on God's promise. Take a moment to declare your faith in God's goodness and trust that He is working behind the scenes.

Speak aloud: "Lord, I trust in Your promises, even when I cannot see the outcome. I believe You are faithful, and I choose to walk by faith, knowing that You are at work in every situation. Thank You for strengthening my faith."

Journaling Prompt:

Reflect on the area of uncertainty or waiting you identified. How does it feel to walk by faith, trusting God without knowing the outcome? Write down any thoughts or emotions as you focus on God's faithfulness.

As you listen, ask God to remind you of His promises. If a specific Scripture or word of encouragement comes to mind, write it down. Remember, God's words of faith and hope will always align with His character and His Word, as we see in 2 Corinthians 5:7: *"For we walk by faith, not by sight."* Let this be a reminder that God is always faithful and His promises are true.

Reflection on the Journey Ahead:

Each step of faith strengthens our trust in God. As you continue this 40-day journey, remember that God's promises are sure and unchanging. He is with you every step of the way, guiding and strengthening your faith.

Day 6 Takeaway:

Today, you practiced walking by faith, trusting in God's promises even when the outcome is unknown. Hold on to His Word and trust that He is working all things for good.

DAY 7: SERVING GOD BY SERVING OTHERS

Scripture Reading:

"For even the Son of Man did not come to be served, but to serve, and to give His life as a ransom for many." —Mark 10:45 (NKJV)

Reflection:

As we conclude this first week, let us turn our focus to serving God by serving others. Jesus Himself set the ultimate example of service, coming not to be served but to serve and to give His life for us. When we serve others with a heart of love and humility, we reflect His character and share His love with the world around us.

One of the most beautiful aspects of serving is when we reach out to those who cannot repay us. This kind of service carries a unique joy—a fulfillment that comes from knowing we are the hands and feet of Jesus, blessing others simply because of God's love in us. *"And you will be blessed, because they cannot repay you; for you shall be repaid at the resurrection of the just"* (Luke 14:14, NKJV). In helping others, especially those who cannot repay, we experience the profound joy that comes from giving freely as God has given us.

Serving does not have to be a grand gesture; it can be as simple as helping a friend, encouraging someone, or lending a listening ear. In doing these things, we not only meet the needs of others but also draw closer to God, who calls us to be His hands and feet. *"As each one has received a gift, minister it to one another, as good stewards of the manifold grace of God"* (1 Peter 4:10, NKJV).

Prayer:

Dear Lord, thank You for Your love and the example of Jesus, who came to serve and give His life for others. Help me to follow in His footsteps, seeking to serve others with a heart of humility and love. Open my eyes to the needs around me, especially those who cannot give back, and show me how I can be a blessing. In Jesus' name, Amen.

Action Step:

Take some time to think of one simple way you can serve someone today, especially someone who may be unable to repay you. It might be encouraging a friend, helping a family member, or reaching out to someone in need. Serving does not have to be complicated—small acts of kindness can make a powerful impact.

Speak aloud: "Lord, thank You for the opportunity to serve. Help me to show Your love through my actions, especially toward those who cannot repay, and let this be a way to glorify You."

Journaling Prompt:

Reflect on the act of service you chose today. How did it feel to reach out in love, especially to someone unable to return the favor? Did you sense God's presence or guidance as you served? Write down any insights or feelings that came up during this time.

Consider asking God to reveal areas where He may want you to serve more consistently. Service often draws us closer to God and others, and it is through these small acts, that His love is shown. *"Let your light so shine before men, that they may see your good works and glorify your Father in heaven"* (Matthew 5:16, NKJV). Serving others glorifies God and helps us grow into the likeness of Christ.

Reflection on the Journey Ahead:

As you continue this 40-day journey, remember that serving others is an essential part of following Christ. Each time you reach out in love, especially to those who cannot repay you, you are sharing God's heart with the world and experiencing the deep joy of giving freely.

Day 7 Takeaway:

Today, you took a step toward serving others in love, following the example of Christ. Remember that each act of service is a way to share God's love, making a difference in ways that only He may see. It's not about seeking recognition or praise but about honoring God. Jesus said, *"But when you do a charitable deed, do not let your left hand know what your right hand is doing, that your charitable deed may be in secret, and your Father who sees in secret will Himself reward you openly"* (Matthew 6:3-4, NKJV).

As you serve, let your goal be for others to say, "Thank God," not "Thank you." Each act of kindness is an opportunity to point others to His love and glory.

DAY 8: EMBRACING HUMILITY

Scripture Reading:

"Humble yourselves in the sight of the Lord, and He will lift you up." —James 4:10 (NKJV)

Reflection:

Today, let us focus on humility, which is central to our walk with God. Humility is not about thinking less of ourselves but recognizing our need for God and placing Him at the center of our lives. It's acknowledging that every gift, every blessing, and every opportunity to serve comes from Him.
When we humble ourselves before God, we open our hearts to His wisdom, His love, and His guidance. Jesus taught humility, showing us what it means to be a servant, even to the point of laying down His life for us. *"Let this mind be in you which was also in Christ Jesus, who... made Himself of no reputation, taking the form of a bondservant"* (Philippians 2:5,7 NKJV). Today, let's ask God to help us embrace a spirit of humility in our thoughts, words, and actions.

Prayer:

Dear Lord, thank You for being my example of humility and love. Help me to let go of pride and to see my life and my blessings as gifts from You. Teach me to humble myself before You, to trust in Your wisdom, and to follow You wholeheartedly. Let my life be a reflection of Your love and grace. In Jesus' name, Amen.

Action Step:

Think of a situation where you might need to practice humility—whether it's letting go of pride in a relationship, asking for help, or choosing to forgive someone. Ask God to guide you in embracing humility, trusting He will lift you up as you honor Him.

Speak aloud: "Lord, I surrender my pride and acknowledge my need for You. Help me to walk in humility, following Jesus' example, and let my life point to You in all I do."

Journaling Prompt:

Reflect on the situation or area in your life where you feel called to practice humility. How does it feel to release pride and trust in God's guidance? Write down any thoughts, struggles, or encouragements you experience as you choose humility.

As you listen, ask God to reveal areas where pride may have taken root in your heart. If He brings something to mind, write it down and ask Him to help you release it. Remember, God's guidance will always lead us to humility and peace, as 1 Peter 5:5 reminds us: *"God resists the proud, but gives grace to the humble."*

Reflection on the Journey Ahead:

Humility strengthens our relationship with God and with others. By choosing humility, we create space for God to work in our lives and through us. As you continue this 40-day journey, let humility guide your actions and thoughts, keeping your heart focused on God and His glory.

Day 8 Takeaway:

Today, you practiced humility, choosing to place God at the center and letting go of pride. Remember, humility allows God to work through you, leading others to see His love and grace. True humility brings honor to God, drawing others closer to Him. When we humble ourselves, God lifts us up, making our lives a testimony of His power and goodness.

DAY 9: BEARING FRUIT IN KEEPING WITH REPENTANCE

Scripture Reading:

"Therefore bear fruits worthy of repentance." —Matthew 3:8 (NKJV)

Reflection:

Today, let us focus on what it means to bear fruit that reflects a heart of repentance. When we live with genuine repentance, it changes not only our hearts but also our impact on the world around us. The *fruit* of our lives is the lasting effect we leave on others—how our actions, words, and choices influence those we encounter.

Jesus called us to live in a way that bears good fruit, which serves as a witness to His transforming power in our lives. John the Baptist emphasized that true repentance should lead to visible change, calling people to *"bear fruits worthy of repentance"* (Matthew 3:8). This means that as we align our lives with God, our actions should demonstrate love, kindness, patience, and humility, showing others the character of Christ.

What kind of fruit is your life bearing? Is it leading others to God, bringing joy and peace, or encouraging others to grow? Or is it causing division, bitterness, or negativity? Today, let's consider the effect of our lives on the world around us, seeking to bear fruit that honors God and blesses others.

Prayer:

Dear Lord, thank You for Your mercy and for leading me to repentance. Help me to live in a way that reflects a true change of heart, bearing fruit that honors You. Show me areas in my life where I can make a positive impact on others. May my life be a reflection of Your love and grace, bringing peace, hope, and encouragement to those around me. In Jesus' name, Amen.

Action Step:

Think about an area in your life where you'd like to see more of God's fruit evident, whether in relationships, habits, or how you handle challenges. Reflect on how your actions in this area affect those around you. Take a moment to ask God to help you bear fruit that leaves a lasting, positive impact on others.

Speak aloud: "Lord, help me to bear fruit that honors You and blesses others. May my life be a reflection of Your love, bringing joy, peace, and encouragement to those around me."

Journaling Prompt:

Reflect on the impact of your actions, words, and choices on others. What kind of fruit is your life producing? How does it feel to consider the effect of your life on the world around you? Write down any insights or areas where you feel called to grow.

As you listen, ask God to reveal ways you can bear more of His fruit, leading others toward Him. Remember, God's desire is for our lives to produce the fruit of His Spirit: *"But the fruit of the Spirit is love, joy, peace, longsuffering, kindness, goodness, faithfulness, gentleness, self-control"* (Galatians 5:22-23, NKJV). The more we align with God, the more our lives will naturally reflect His presence, leaving an impact on others.

Reflection on the Journey Ahead:

Bearing fruit that keeps with repentance is about more than personal change; it's about creating a ripple effect that blesses others and draws them to God. Each day we walk with God, our actions and attitudes can leave a lasting impression, showing others His love. As you continue this 40-day journey, let your life be a testimony of God's grace, impacting the world in meaningful ways.

Day 9 Takeaway:

Today, you took a step toward bearing fruit that honors God, reflecting His presence in a way that blesses others. Remember, the fruit of your life is the impact you have on the world around you. As you continue to grow, ask yourself what legacy you want to leave. Each day is an opportunity to let your life point others to God and to bear fruit that has a lasting, positive effect.

DAY 10: CELEBRATING TRANSFORMATION AND RENEWAL

Scripture Reading:

"And do not be conformed to this world, but be transformed by the renewing of your mind, that you may prove what is that good and acceptable and perfect will of God." —Romans 12:2 (NKJV)

Reflection:

Today marks a significant step in our journey together: we're 25 percent through this time of transformation. As you reflect on the past 10 days, think about how God has already been working in your heart and mind. Transformation is not always a sudden change; it is often a gradual process that happens as we commit to seeking God, listening to His voice, and aligning our lives with His will.

Romans 12:2 reminds us that transformation begins with the **renewal of our minds**. As we dedicate time to God each day, He renews our thoughts, desires, and actions, making us more like Christ. Even in the small changes—choosing kindness, seeking humility, practicing gratitude—God's transformative work is evident. Today, let's celebrate what He is already done and look forward to what He will continue to do in the days ahead.

Prayer:

Dear Lord, thank You for your work in my life. As I look back on these past 10 days, I see Your hand guiding and shaping me. Continue to transform my heart and renew my mind, that I may live according to Your perfect will. Help me trust Your process, knowing that You are faithful in completing the work You've begun. In Jesus' name, Amen.

Action Step:

Take a moment to reflect on one area where you've already noticed growth or change. Write down how God has been at work in this area, no matter how small it may seem. As you recognize His hand in your life, celebrate this transformation and commit to the journey ahead with renewed focus.
Speak aloud: "Lord, thank You for the transformation You've begun in me. I trust You will continue this work, renewing my heart and mind daily. May my life be a reflection of Your perfect will."

Journaling Prompt:

Reflect on the journey so far. What changes have you noticed in your thoughts, actions, or relationships? How has God been speaking to you over these past 10 days? Write down any specific moments or lessons that stand out, thanking God for the progress He has already brought about.
As you journal, ask God to reveal areas where He wants to continue working in your life. Transformation is a journey, and each step brings us closer to His purpose. *"Being confident of this very thing, that He who has begun a good work in you will complete it until the day of Jesus Christ"* (Philippians 1:6, NKJV). Trust that God is faithful in continuing what He has started.

Reflection on the Journey Ahead:

Transformation is an ongoing process, and each day brings new opportunities to grow closer to God. As we reach this milestone, let it serve as a reminder that God is constantly renewing our hearts and minds, shaping us for His purpose. The journey is not always easy, but we are being made more like Christ with each step.

Day 10 Takeaway:

Today, you celebrated a milestone in your journey of transformation. Remember that God's work in you is ongoing—He is faithful, and He will continue to renew and shape you as you seek Him. Embrace the journey ahead, confident that God is bringing about His perfect will in your life.

DAY 11: PERSEVERING IN FAITHFULNESS

Scripture Reading:

"Let us not grow weary while doing good, for in due season we shall reap if we do not lose heart." —Galatians 6:9 (NKJV)

"Behold, to obey is better than sacrifice, and to heed than the fat of rams." —1 Samuel 15:22 (NKJV)

Reflection:

As we enter the second quarter of this journey, it is a good time to focus on perseverance and faithful obedience. Spiritual growth is not always easy; sometimes, we may feel discouraged or wonder if the effort we are putting in makes a difference. Galatians 6:9 reminds us to hold fast and continue doing good, trusting that in time, God's work in us will bear fruit.
God values our faithful obedience above all else. As 1 Samuel 15:22 reminds us, *"to obey is better than sacrifice."* God doesn't desire empty actions but a heart committed to following His ways. Perseverance requires faithfulness and patience, especially when the changes we're seeking in our lives aren't immediately visible. But God sees every small act of obedience and every moment spent in His presence. Today, let's commit to obedience and faithfulness, trusting that God's work in us is constant, even when unseen. Each step of obedience brings us closer to His purpose.

Prayer:

Dear Lord, thank You for Your faithfulness and for the work You are doing in my life. Help me to persevere in this journey, trusting that You are with me every step of the way. Strengthen my heart and renew my commitment to obey and seek You daily. May I find joy in knowing that You are faithful in completing the work You have begun. In Jesus' name, Amen.

Action Step:

Think about one area where perseverance in obedience is challenging for you—whether it is in prayer, in overcoming a habit, or in another area of growth. Ask God for strength to stay faithful, even when progress feels slow or difficult, knowing He delights in your obedience.
Speak aloud: "Lord, I commit to faithfulness and obedience. Help me to press on in my journey with You, trusting that each step brings me closer to Your purpose for my life."

Journaling Prompt:

Reflect on an area in your spiritual journey where it is difficult to stay committed in obedience. How can you remind yourself of God's faithfulness in these moments? Write down any thoughts, struggles, or encouragements as you commit to persevering in this area.
As you journal, ask God for encouragement and strength. Remember, God is faithful to bring you through, as He promises in James 1:12: *"Blessed is the man who endures temptation; for when he has been approved, he will receive the crown of life which the Lord has promised to those who love Him."* Let this reminder encourage you to keep pressing forward.

Reflection on the Journey Ahead:

Perseverance and obedience are essential in the journey of faith, and every day you continue seeking God is a day closer to His purpose. Remember, transformation happens over time, and God is patient, leading us step by step. As you continue this 40-day journey, lean on His strength, knowing He is with you every step of the way.

Day 11 Takeaway:

Today, you committed to perseverance and obedience, trusting that God's work in you will bear fruit in time. Remember that each step of faithfulness builds resilience and strengthens your connection to God. Keep pressing forward with hope, knowing that God values your obedience and will complete His work in you.

DAY 12: RENEWING YOUR COMMITMENT

Scripture Reading:

"Commit your way to the Lord, trust also in Him, and He shall bring it to pass." — Psalm 37:5 (NKJV)

Reflection:

Today, let's take time to renew our commitment to God's purposes in our lives. This journey of transformation is filled with moments that challenge, stretch, and inspire us. As we seek to grow closer to God, we must recommit regularly, renewing our dedication to Him. Psalm 37:5 reminds us to commit our ways to the Lord and trust He will bring about His purposes in our lives. Committing to God means surrendering our plans, desires, and fears, trusting that He will guide us. Each time we renew our commitment, we declare our faith in God's ability to work in and through us, no matter what challenges we face. Today, let's recommit to walking in God's ways, trusting that He will strengthen and sustain us every step of the way.

Prayer:

Dear Lord, today I renew my commitment to You. Thank You for walking with me on this journey and for shaping me according to Your purpose. Help me to trust in You completely, surrendering my plans and desires into Your hands. Strengthen my heart and help me to follow You faithfully. I commit my way to You, Lord, knowing You will bring it to pass. In Jesus' name, Amen.

Action Step:

Take a few moments to think about any specific areas where you may need to renew your commitment to God's will—whether in prayer, trusting His timing, or letting go of personal ambitions. As you identify these areas, recommit them to God, asking Him to guide and strengthen you.
Speak aloud*:* "Lord, I renew my commitment to You today. I trust You with my plans, my life, and my journey. Help me to stay faithful and to walk in Your ways."

Journaling Prompt:

Reflect on the areas where you've renewed your commitment today. Are there places where you feel God is calling you to trust Him more deeply? Write down any insights, thoughts, or encouragements that come as you dedicate these areas to Him.
As you journal, remind yourself that God's promises are true and that He will bring His work in you to completion. *"The Lord will perfect that which concerns me; Your mercy, O Lord, endures forever"* (Psalm 138:8, NKJV). God's love for you is constant, and He is committed to seeing His purpose fulfilled in your life.

Reflection on the Journey Ahead:

Renewing your commitment to God's will is a powerful step in your journey of transformation. Each time you recommit, you reaffirm your trust in His love and guidance. As you continue this 40-day journey, remember that God is faithful and that He delights in your desire to follow Him wholeheartedly.

Day 12 Takeaway:
Today, you renewed your commitment to God's purpose in your life. Remember that each step of dedication strengthens your connection to God and brings you closer to His will. Keep trusting that He will bring about His perfect work in you as you continue this journey.

DAY 13: SURRENDERING CONTROL

Scripture Reading:
"Cast your burden on the Lord, and He shall sustain you; He shall never permit the righteous to be moved." —Psalm 55:22 (NKJV)

Reflection:
Today, we are focusing on surrendering control to God. It's natural to want to hold on tightly to our plans, dreams, and even fears, but God invites us to cast our burdens on Him, trusting that He will sustain us. Psalm 55:22 reminds us that we don't have to carry our worries and burdens alone. Instead, God calls us to release them into His hands, promising to sustain and strengthen us in return.

Surrendering control is an act of faith that says, "God, I believe Your ways are higher than mine." It requires humility, acknowledging that we don't always know what's best, but God does. Today, let's take a step of faith by surrendering those areas where we might be holding on too tightly. When we let go, we allow God to work in ways that go beyond our own abilities and understanding.

Prayer:
Dear Lord, thank You for being my guide and my strength. Help me to let go of my need to control every detail of my life and to trust You with all my heart. I surrender my plans, my worries, and my desires to You, believing that Your ways are perfect. Teach me to rely on You completely, knowing that You are directing my path. In Jesus' name, Amen.

Action Step:
Take a moment to identify one specific area where you're struggling to surrender control—whether it's a decision, a relationship, or a worry about the future. Commit this area to God, letting go of your need to manage the outcome and trusting Him to lead you.

Speak aloud: "Lord, I surrender this part of my life to You. Help me to trust that You know what's best, and I believe that You are working for my good."

Journaling Prompt:
Reflect on how it feels to let go of control in this area of your life. Are there fears or concerns as you surrender it to God? Write down any thoughts, emotions, or encouragements you feel as you release control.
As you listen, remember that God's guidance will always align with His promises. *"For My thoughts are not your thoughts, nor are your ways My ways," says the Lord* (Isaiah 55:8, NKJV). Trusting in God's wisdom means believing that He sees the bigger picture, even when we don't. Let today be a reminder that His plan is always greater than our own.

Reflection on the Journey Ahead:
Surrendering control is not a one-time act but a daily decision to trust God. Each time you release an area of your life to Him, you choose faith over fear and open your heart to His perfect will. As you continue this 40-day journey, let go of what you're holding tightly, and let God guide you into a future shaped by His love and wisdom.

Day 13 Takeaway:

Today, you took a step in surrendering control, trusting that God's ways are higher than your own. Remember that true peace comes not from controlling every outcome but from releasing your life into God's hands. He is faithful and He will lead you every step of the way.

DAY 14: CULTIVATING PEACE THROUGH TRUST

Scripture Reading:
"You will keep him in perfect peace, whose mind is stayed on You, because he trusts in You." —Isaiah 26:3 (NKJV)

Reflection:
Today, we focus on finding peace through trust in God. Peace can seem elusive in a world filled with distractions, stress, and worry. Yet, God promises "perfect peace" to those whose minds are steadfastly fixed on Him. Isaiah 26:3 reminds us that peace isn't something we create on our own—it's a gift from God that comes as we place our trust fully in Him.

True peace doesn't come from perfect circumstances; it comes from knowing that God is in control. By surrendering our anxieties and focusing on God's promises, we can experience His peace that goes beyond human understanding. Today, let's practice trusting God with our worries and resting in His assurance, allowing His perfect peace to fill our hearts.

Prayer:
Dear Lord, thank You for the peace You offer me. Help me to keep my mind and heart focused on You, trusting that You are in control. Teach me to release my worries to You, knowing that You care for me. May Your peace fill my heart and guard my thoughts, reminding me that You are with me in every moment. In Jesus' name, Amen.

Action Step:
Identify one or two things that often disrupt your sense of peace—worries, situations, or thoughts. Take a moment to consciously hand these over to God, asking Him to replace your anxiety with His peace.

Speak aloud: "Lord, I release my worries to You. Help me to trust You completely and to rest in the perfect peace that only You can provide."

Journaling Prompt:
Reflect on how it feels to release your worries and allow God's peace to fill your heart. Are there specific areas where you find it challenging to let go? Write down any thoughts or insights as you focus on peace through trust in God.

As you listen, remember that peace is a gift from God, not something you have to earn. Jesus assures us in John 14:27, *"Peace I leave with you, My peace I give to you; not as the world gives do I give to you. Let not your heart be troubled, neither let it be afraid."* Let this reminder fill you with confidence that His peace is ever-present.

Reflection on the Journey Ahead:
Cultivating peace is a lifelong journey of learning to trust God more fully. Each time you place your worries in His hands, you choose to walk in faith and embrace His promise of peace. As you continue this 40-day journey, let His peace guide you, knowing He is with you through every step.

Day 14 Takeaway:

Today, you took a step toward experiencing God's perfect peace, trusting Him with your worries. Remember that peace comes from releasing control and focusing on God's presence. In every moment, His peace is available to you, calming your heart and guiding you through life's challenges.

DAY 15: CELEBRATING PROGRESS WITH JOY

Scripture Reading:
"This is the day the Lord has made; we will rejoice and be glad in it." —Psalm 118:24 (NKJV)

Reflection:
Today, we celebrate our progress and rejoice in the steps we've taken so far. Psalm 118:24 reminds us that each day is a gift from God and an opportunity to find joy in His presence. While we may not be halfway through, we're making great strides, and each day brings us closer to God's purpose for us. Celebrating our progress renews our energy and builds our faith. It is not about having reached the destination but about recognizing God's work along the way. Every step, every prayer, and every change bring us closer to His heart. So today, let us pause, reflect, and rejoice in the progress made, knowing that God is with us every step of the journey.

Prayer:
Dear Lord, thank You for each step of this journey. I rejoice in the progress You're helping me make, and I am grateful for Your presence, guidance, and love. Help me to continue with joy and perseverance, knowing that You are faithful to complete the work You've started. I celebrate Your goodness today and look forward with excitement to the days ahead. In Jesus' name, Amen.

Action Step:
Take a moment to celebrate something specific from this journey so far—a small victory, a moment of clarity, or a feeling of peace. Think about how you've seen God working and let yourself feel joy for the progress He's helping you make.

Speak aloud: "Lord, I celebrate the progress we've made together. Thank You for guiding me, strengthening me, and walking with me on this journey. I look forward to each step with joy, knowing You are by my side."

Journaling Prompt:
Reflect on the growth you've experienced over these past 15 days. What changes, big or small, have you noticed? How have your faith and trust in God deepened? Write down what you're grateful for and celebrate each victory as part of God's work in you.

As you journal, remember Philippians 4:4: *"Rejoice in the Lord always. Again I will say, rejoice!"* Let this be a reminder that God delights in your progress, no matter where you are on the journey. Rejoice in His faithfulness and in the steps you've taken together.

Reflection on the Journey Ahead:
Celebrating along the way reminds us of God's presence in every moment. Each step brings us closer to His purpose and strengthens our faith. As you continue this 40-day journey, carry this joy with you, trusting that God will continue His work in you. Rejoice in what has been accomplished, and look forward with hope to what lies ahead.

Day 15 Takeaway:

Today, you took a moment to celebrate your progress, rejoicing in God's faithfulness on this journey. Remember to carry this joy forward, allowing it to renew your energy and strengthen your faith. Each step brings you closer to Him, and He delights in every part of your journey.

DAY 16: PROTECTING SACRED TIME WITH GOD

Scripture Reading:
"Be still, and know that I am God." —Psalm 46:10 (NKJV)

Reflection:
Today, let us focus on the importance of treating time with God as sacred and protecting it from distractions. In a world full of noise, demands, and busyness, God calls us to *"be still"* (Psalm 46:10), inviting us to rest and connect with Him.

Jesus is our true Sabbath—He is the source of deep, spiritual rest that goes beyond a single day of the week. In Him, we find peace for our souls, freedom from striving, and comfort in knowing that we are fully accepted and loved by God. Just as God intended the Sabbath to be a time of rest, Jesus offers us rest every day as we come to Him.

We create space to recharge, gain clarity, and find renewal by protecting this sacred time. Jesus invites us to lay down our burdens and rest in Him. When we quiet our minds and set aside distractions, we show that we value Him above all else. Today, let's commit to making time with God a protected, sacred part of our day—a source of peace, guidance, and strength.

Prayer:
Dear Lord, help me to guard my time with You as sacred. I want to find rest in Your presence, knowing You are my true Sabbath. Teach me to set aside distractions and be still, allowing Your peace to fill my heart. Thank You for inviting me into Your rest and for meeting me here. In Jesus' name, Amen.

Action Step:
Set aside a specific time today to rest in God's presence. Find a quiet space, free from distractions, and allow yourself to truly rest in Him. Remember that Jesus is your Sabbath, the One who brings lasting peace and rest to your soul. **Speak aloud**: "Lord, I come to You as my true Sabbath, trusting You for peace and rest. Help me to let go of distractions and to be fully present in Your presence."

Journaling Prompt:
Reflect on what it feels like to find rest in Jesus as your Sabbath. How does spending undistracted time with Him impact your heart and mind? Write down any thoughts or insights that come as you allow yourself to rest in Him. As you journal, remember Jesus' words in Matthew 11:28: *"Come to Me, all you who labor and are heavy laden, and I will give you rest."* Let this remind you that God calls you to find true rest in Him, not just as a momentary pause, but as a daily renewal of peace and joy.

Reflection on the Journey Ahead:
Jesus offers you rest and renewal each day, calling you to come to Him and find peace for your soul. As you continue this journey, let your moments with Him be a source of refreshment and strength, trusting that He is your true Sabbath. By making time for Him, you are building a lasting foundation of faith and finding true rest.

Day 16 Takeaway:

Today, you committed to protecting sacred time with God, finding rest in Jesus as your true Sabbath. Remember that these moments with Him are essential, a source of peace and strength to guide you each day. Let this time in His presence draw you closer to Him, deepening your relationship and filling your heart with His peace.

DAY 17: CULTIVATING GRATITUDE AS A PATHWAY TO JOY

Scripture Reading:
"In everything give thanks; for this is the will of God in Christ Jesus for you." —1 Thessalonians 5:18 (NKJV)

Reflection:
Today, let us focus on cultivating gratitude as a way to experience deeper joy in God. 1 Thessalonians 5:18 encourages us to give thanks "in everything." When we practice gratitude daily, we begin to see God's hand at work in every area of our lives—both in blessings and even in challenges.

Gratitude is a powerful tool that transforms our outlook. When we pause to thank God for His presence, His love, and His guidance, we open ourselves to a joy that doesn't depend on circumstances. It redirects our focus from what we may lack to what we already have in Him. Today, let's allow gratitude to draw us closer to God, filling our hearts with joy and helping us see the beauty in every moment.

Prayer:
Dear Lord, thank You for Your endless blessings and for being with me through every moment of my life. Help me cultivate a grateful heart, recognizing Your goodness in all things. Teach me to see even my challenges as opportunities to grow closer to You. Let my gratitude bring me joy, reminding me that You are faithful and that Your love is constant. In Jesus' name, Amen.

Action Step:
Take time to list five things you're thankful for today. As you write each one, pause to thank God for it, allowing gratitude to fill your heart. These can be big blessings or small moments that bring you joy.

Speak aloud*:* "Lord, thank You for Your goodness. I am grateful for each blessing You have given me, and I choose to rejoice in Your love and faithfulness."

Journaling Prompt:
Reflect on the impact of gratitude in your life. How does focusing on gratitude affect your attitude, outlook, or relationship with God? Write down any thoughts or experiences that come as you intentionally choose thankfulness today.

As you journal, remember James 1:17: *"Every good gift and every perfect gift is from above, and comes down from the Father of lights."* Let this remind you that each blessing in your life, no matter how small, is a gift from God.

Reflection on the Journey Ahead:
Gratitude is a practice that leads to joy, reminding us of God's faithfulness and grace. As you continue this journey, make gratitude a daily habit, allowing it to draw you closer to God and fill your life with His joy. The more we thank God, the more we recognize His constant presence and love in every moment.

Day 17 Takeaway:

Today, you practiced gratitude, choosing to see God's blessings in your life. Remember that gratitude leads to joy, filling your heart with peace and helping you experience God's presence more fully. Let this habit become a way to stay connected to Him and experience His goodness every day.

DAY 18: EMBRACING FORGIVENESS

Scripture Reading:
"And be kind to one another, tenderhearted, forgiving one another, even as God in Christ forgave you." —Ephesians 4:32 (NKJV)

Reflection:
Today, we focus on forgiveness—a powerful act that brings freedom and healing to our hearts. Ephesians 4:32 reminds us to forgive as God has forgiven us. Forgiveness isn't always easy, but it's essential for spiritual growth and peace. When we choose to forgive, we're letting go of the hurts and resentments that weigh us down, making room for God's love and joy. Forgiveness doesn't mean that what happened was okay or that we ignore the pain it caused; it means we're choosing to release it to God, trusting Him to bring justice and healing. Today, let's reflect on the freedom that forgiveness offers, both to ourselves and to others. By forgiving, we mirror the grace God has shown us, opening our hearts to a deeper connection with Him.

Prayer:
Dear Lord, thank You for the gift of forgiveness that You've extended to me through Jesus. Help me to forgive others as You have forgiven me. I surrender any hurt, resentment, or bitterness that I may be holding onto, trusting You to bring healing and peace. Teach me to forgive with a tender heart, allowing Your love to fill me. In Jesus' name, Amen.

Action Step:
Consider if there's someone you need to forgive or a past hurt you need to release. Write their name on a piece of paper and say a prayer, asking God to help you forgive them fully. Then, tear up or dispose of the paper as a symbol of releasing that hurt to God.
Speak aloud: "Lord, I choose to forgive and let go of this hurt. Fill my heart with Your peace and help me to walk in freedom."

Journaling Prompt:
Reflect on the process of forgiveness. How does letting go of resentment make you feel? Are there specific people or situations where forgiveness has been difficult? Write down any thoughts or struggles, asking God to help you release any lingering hurt.

As you journal, remember Jesus' words in Matthew 6:14-15: *"For if you forgive men their trespasses, your heavenly Father will also forgive you. But if you do not forgive men their trespasses, neither will your Father forgive your trespasses."* Let this reminder encourage you to extend the same grace to others that God has shown to you.

Reflection on the Journey Ahead:
Forgiveness is an essential part of our walk with God, freeing us from the chains of resentment and bitterness. As you continue this journey, make forgiveness a regular practice, knowing that God's love and peace will fill the spaces where hurt once resided. Forgiving others brings freedom and deepens your relationship with God.

Day 18 Takeaway:

Today, you took a step toward embracing forgiveness, choosing to let go of past hurts. Remember that forgiveness brings freedom and peace, opening your heart to experience God's love more fully. Let this act of grace draw you closer to Him and fill your heart with His peace.

DAY 19: EMBRACING GOD'S HEALING

Scripture Reading:
"Heal me, O Lord, and I shall be healed; save me, and I shall be saved, for You are my praise." —Jeremiah 17:14 (NKJV)

Reflection:
Today, we focus on God's power to heal. Healing is more than just physical—it's a process of restoration in our minds, emotions, and spirits. Jeremiah 17:14 captures a heartfelt cry for healing, showing us that God is both able and willing to bring wholeness into our lives. Whether we're dealing with past hurts, emotional wounds, or physical needs, God invites us to bring our brokenness to Him, trusting in His power to restore us.

Healing is often a journey, and sometimes it takes time. But as we open our hearts to God and seek His presence, He begins to mend what's been broken. Today, let's bring our needs to God, trusting that He sees every wound and desires to make us whole.

Prayer:
Dear Lord, thank You for being my healer. I come to You today with an open heart, asking for Your healing touch in every area of my life. Restore me in body, mind, and spirit, and help me to trust in Your timing and process. Let Your peace fill me, and may Your strength sustain me as I walk this journey of healing. In Jesus' name, Amen.

Action Step:
Take time today to identify one area of your life where you need healing. This could be physical, emotional, or spiritual. Write down a short prayer asking God to bring healing and restoration to this area, and thank Him in advance for His love and power to make you whole.
Speak aloud: "Lord, I trust in Your power to heal. Thank You for working in my life and bringing restoration to my heart."

Journaling Prompt:
Reflect on the areas in your life where you need healing. Are there specific hurts, pains, or struggles that you've carried for too long? Write down any thoughts or feelings that arise as you invite God into these areas of brokenness, and thank Him for being your healer.
As you journal, remember Psalm 147:3: *"He heals the brokenhearted and binds up their wounds."* Let this remind you that God sees every wound, and He is faithful to bring healing and comfort.

Reflection on the Journey Ahead:
Healing is a journey that often requires patience and trust. Each time you bring your needs to God, you're allowing Him to work in your heart and life, bringing about His perfect peace. As you continue this journey, trust in God's power to heal, restore, and make you whole.

Day 19 Takeaway:

Today, you took a step toward embracing God's healing, trusting Him to bring restoration to every area of your life. Remember that healing is a journey, and God is with you every step of the way. Allow His peace and strength to sustain you as you trust in His faithful love.

DAY 20: FAITHFULNESS IN SMALL STEPS

Scripture Reading:
"His lord said to him, 'Well done, good and faithful servant; you were faithful over a few things, I will make you ruler over many things. Enter into the joy of your lord.'" —
Matthew 25:23 (NKJV)

Reflection:
Today marks the halfway point of our journey, a time to pause and reflect on the value of faithfulness in small steps. In Matthew 25:23, Jesus tells the story of a servant who was faithful with what he was given, showing that even seemingly small acts of obedience have great significance. As we tithe our time, serve others, and dedicate ourselves to prayer, it's the consistency, not the size of the action, that builds our relationship with God.

Small acts of faithfulness—whether it's a short prayer, a moment of gratitude, or a small act of kindness—are valuable in God's eyes. They shape us over time, drawing us closer to Him and transforming our hearts. Today, let's celebrate every small step we've taken and commit to remaining faithful in the days ahead, trusting that God sees each act of dedication and honors our journey.

Prayer:
Dear Lord, thank You for valuing each small act of faithfulness. Help me to remain committed to the small steps of service, prayer, and gratitude, trusting that they draw me closer to You. Teach me to see each moment as an opportunity to serve and honor You. Thank You for Your faithfulness to me, and help me to be faithful to You in return. In Jesus' name, Amen.

Action Step:
Reflect on a few small but meaningful actions you can continue to do each day to grow in your walk with God—whether it's a moment of prayer, reading a Bible verse, or showing kindness to someone. Choose one or two to focus on consistently as you move forward in this journey.

Speak aloud: "Lord, I choose to be faithful in small steps, trusting that You see and value every act of service and prayer."

Journaling Prompt:
Think back over the first 20 days of this journey. What small steps of faithfulness have been most meaningful to you? How have these small, consistent acts shaped your relationship with God? Write down any insights or areas where you feel called to remain faithful, celebrating how far you've come.

As you journal, remember Galatians 6:9: *"And let us not grow weary while doing good, for in due season we shall reap if we do not lose heart."* Let this encourage you that each step, no matter how small, is part of God's greater plan for your life.

Reflection on the Journey Ahead:
Faithfulness in small steps is a powerful way to grow in God. As you continue this journey, remember that every act of dedication—no matter how small—is seen by God and helps build a foundation of faith and trust. Let these small, consistent steps draw you closer to Him and bring you joy in the journey.

Day 20 Takeaway:

Today, you celebrated faithfulness in small steps, recognizing that each moment spent in service, prayer, or gratitude is meaningful to God. As you continue, let these consistent acts deepen your relationship with Him and remind you that He values every step of faithfulness.

DAY 21: RENEWING YOUR PERSPECTIVE

Scripture Reading:
"Set your mind on things above, not on things on the earth." —Colossians 3:2 (NKJV)

Reflection:
Today, let's focus on renewing our perspective by setting our minds on things above. Colossians 3:2 encourages us to look beyond earthly concerns, fixing our focus on God's eternal truths. When we align our thoughts with God's, we find peace and clarity that the world cannot offer. This shift in perspective allows us to see our lives in light of God's purpose and to trust that He is always at work, even when we don't understand everything that happens. Renewing our perspective means lifting our eyes from immediate circumstances to see the bigger picture that God sees. It reminds us that we're part of a much greater story, one shaped by His love and wisdom. Today, let's ask God to align our thoughts with His, helping us to walk in faith and embrace the joy that comes from looking to Him.

Prayer:
Dear Lord, thank You for calling me to set my mind on things above. Help me to renew my perspective and see my life through Your eyes. Align my thoughts with Your truth and remind me of Your eternal purpose. Teach me to trust in Your wisdom, finding peace and joy in the knowledge that You hold all things together. In Jesus' name, Amen.

Action Step:
Think of an area in your life where your perspective might be limited by earthly concerns or worries. Bring it before God, asking Him to help you view it through His eternal lens, allowing His truth to bring peace and understanding.

Speak aloud*:* "Lord, I set my mind on things above. Help me to see my life and my circumstances from Your perspective and to trust in Your perfect plan."

Journaling Prompt:
Reflect on areas where you feel challenged to keep a heavenly perspective. How would your thoughts or actions change if you focused on God's eternal truths rather than immediate concerns? As you ask God to renew your perspective, write down any insights or encouragements.

As you journal, remember Philippians 4:8: *"Finally, brethren, whatever things are true, whatever things are noble, whatever things are just, whatever things are pure, whatever things are lovely, whatever things are of good report, if there is any virtue and if there is anything praiseworthy—meditate on these things."* Let this verse remind you to keep your mind focused on God's goodness and His eternal purposes.

Reflection on the Journey Ahead:
Renewing your perspective is a powerful way to deepen your faith and find joy in God's purpose for you. As you continue this journey, let God shape your thoughts, helping you see life through His eternal lens. Trust that each step, aligned with His truth, brings peace and clarity.

Day 21 Takeaway:

Today, you focused on setting your mind on things above, allowing God's eternal perspective to shape your outlook. Remember that aligning your thoughts with God's brings peace and a deeper sense of purpose. Let His truths guide you as you continue this journey of faith.

DAY 22: SERVING OTHERS WITH HUMILITY

Scripture Reading:
"For even the Son of Man did not come to be served, but to serve, and to give His life a ransom for many." —Mark 10:45 (NKJV)

Reflection:
Today, let's focus on serving others with humility, following the example Jesus set for us. Mark 10:45 reminds us that Jesus, the Son of God, came not to be served but to serve. His life was a demonstration of love, compassion, and humility, showing us that true greatness is found in serving others.

When we serve with humility, we reflect God's love in tangible ways, meeting the needs of those around us and letting our actions speak of His grace. Serving others isn't about recognition; it's about honoring God by giving of ourselves to those in need. Today, let's look for opportunities to serve others, big or small, and to do so with a heart focused on love and humility.

Prayer:
Dear Lord, thank You for the example of Jesus, who served with humility and love. Help me to follow in His footsteps, serving others with a humble heart and a desire to show Your love. May my actions reflect Your grace, and may I find joy in giving of myself to others. Let my service be an offering to You, bringing honor to Your name. In Jesus' name, Amen.

Action Step:
Seek out an opportunity to serve someone today—whether it is through a kind word, a helping hand, or a small act of generosity. As you serve, keep your focus on reflecting God's love and humility, remembering that true service is done quietly, without seeking recognition.

Speak aloud: "Lord, help me to serve others with humility and love, following Jesus' example of selfless service."

Journaling Prompt:
Reflect on the idea of humble service. What does it mean to serve others without expecting anything in return? How can serving others draw you closer to God? Write down any thoughts or insights as you consider the importance of humility in your actions.

As you journal, remember Philippians 2:3-4: *"Let nothing be done through selfish ambition or conceit, but in lowliness of mind let each esteem others better than himself. Let each of you look out not only for his own interests, but also for the interests of others."* Let this encourage you to serve with a heart focused on others, prioritizing their needs over your own.

Reflection on the Journey Ahead:
Serving others with humility brings us closer to God's heart, helping us to grow in compassion and selflessness. As you continue this journey, let each act of service be a reflection of God's love, building a habit of humble giving that honors Him. Embrace the joy that comes from putting others before yourself.

Day 22 Takeaway:
Today, you focused on humbly serving others, reflecting God's love through your actions. Remember that true service is done quietly, with a humble heart that seeks to honor God. Let each act of kindness draw you closer to Him and build a spirit of selflessness.

DAY 23: STEPPING OUT OF YOUR COMFORT ZONE TO SERVE JESUS

Scripture Reading:
"And He said to them all, 'If anyone desires to come after Me, let him deny himself, and take up his cross daily, and follow Me.'" —Luke 9:23 (NKJV)

Reflection:
Today, let's focus on stepping out of our comfort zones to serve Jesus. Following Jesus often involves doing things that challenge us, stretch us, and lead us into unfamiliar territory. Luke 9:23 reminds us that following Christ means denying ourselves and taking up our cross daily, embracing whatever He calls us to, even if it feels uncomfortable.

Stepping out of our comfort zone could mean having a difficult conversation, helping someone in need, sharing our faith openly, or volunteering in a new area. These acts may feel intimidating, but they are opportunities to trust God's strength instead of our own. Today, let's embrace the challenge, knowing that God will use these moments to grow our faith and help us become more like Christ.

Prayer:
Dear Lord, thank You for calling me to follow You wholeheartedly. Help me to step out of my comfort zone and serve You with courage. Give me strength to trust in Your power and not my own abilities. Remind me that every challenge is an opportunity to draw closer to You and to serve others in Your name. Guide me as I take this step of faith, and use it to grow me. In Jesus' name, Amen.

Action Step:
Identify one specific way you can step out of your comfort zone to serve Jesus today. This could be speaking a kind word to someone you don't know, sharing your faith, volunteering in a new capacity, or helping someone in need. Take a step of faith, trusting that God will be with you as you serve.
Speak aloud: "Lord, I am willing to step out of my comfort zone to serve You. Give me the courage and strength to follow where You lead, trusting that You are with me."

Journaling Prompt:
Reflect on any fears, hesitations, or excitement you feel about stepping out of your comfort zone. How might this challenge help you grow in your faith and trust in God? Write down any thoughts or insights as you take this step to serve Jesus in a new way.

As you journal, remember 2 Corinthians 12:9: *"And He said to me, 'My grace is sufficient for you, for My strength is made perfect in weakness.'"* Let this verse encourage you to rely on God's strength as you serve, knowing that He is with you every step of the way.

Reflection on the Journey Ahead:
Stepping out of our comfort zones helps us grow in courage, humility, and faith. As you continue this journey, trust that each challenge is an opportunity to rely on God more fully and to serve Him with a willing heart. Embrace these moments as steps toward becoming more like Christ.

Day 23 Takeaway:

Today, you embraced the challenge of stepping out of your comfort zone to serve Jesus. Remember that every step of faith deepens your relationship with Him and helps you grow in strength and courage. Trust in God's presence as you continue serving Him in new ways.

DAY 24: EMBRACING FAITH WITH CHILDLIKE TRUST

Scripture Reading:
"I know your works. See, I have set before you an open door, and no one can shut it; for you have a little strength, have kept My word, and have not denied My name." —Revelation 3:8 (NKJV)

Reflection:
Today, let's focus on holding fast to our faith, approaching God with childlike trust, and never denying His name. Revelation 3:8 reminds us that God opens doors no one can shut, and He honors our faithfulness, even when our strength feels small. Like children who come to their parents with simple, unwavering trust, we are invited to come to God with openness and humility, fully believing in His love and power.

Jesus taught us to have a childlike faith—one that is free from doubt, open-hearted, and curious about the wonders of God. When we approach Him in this way, we experience a deeper connection, finding joy and peace in His presence. Today, let us recommit to coming to God without fear or hesitation, trusting in His goodness and standing firm in our faith, knowing He honors those who do not deny His name.

Prayer:
Dear Lord, thank You for the invitation to come to You with childlike faith. Help me to trust in Your goodness and to approach You with openness and joy. Strengthen my heart to never deny Your name but to stand firm in my faith. Remind me that You open doors no one can shut, and guide me as I walk through them with faith and courage. In Jesus' name, Amen.

Action Step:
Take a moment today to reflect on the simplicity of childlike faith. Approach God with openness—talk to Him, ask questions, and listen for His guidance. Let go of any fear or hesitation, trusting fully in His love for you.

Speak aloud: "Lord, I come to You with childlike faith, trusting in Your goodness and rejoicing in Your love. Strengthen me to stand firm and to never deny Your name."

Journaling Prompt:
Reflect on what it means to come to God with childlike faith. Are there areas in your life where you feel hesitant or struggle with doubt? How might approaching God with openness and trust help you grow in faith? Write down any thoughts, questions, or insights as you open your heart to Him.

As you journal, remember Matthew 18:3: *"Assuredly, I say to you, unless you are converted and become as little children, you will by no means enter the kingdom of heaven."* Let this verse remind you of the importance of trusting God with a heart that is open, joyful, and full of wonder.

Reflection on the Journey Ahead:
Childlike faith draws us closer to God, helping us to find joy and peace in His presence. As you continue this journey, remember that God values your trust and openness. Stand firm in your faith, knowing that He honors those who do not deny His name and rewards those who seek Him with a child's heart.

Day 24 Takeaway:

Today, you embraced childlike faith and reaffirmed your commitment to stand firm in God's name. Remember that trusting God like a child brings you closer to Him and opens doors that only He can open. Let this simple, joyful faith guide you each day as you walk with Him.

DAY 25: BUILDING A STRONG FOUNDATION IN GOD'S WORD

Scripture Reading:
"Therefore whoever hears these sayings of Mine, and does them, I will liken him to a wise man who built his house on the rock." —Matthew 7:24 (NKJV)

Reflection:
Today, let's focus on building a strong foundation in God's Word. In Matthew 7:24, Jesus compares those who hear and apply His teachings to a wise builder who builds on solid rock. When we anchor our lives in God's Word, we gain wisdom, strength, and stability, allowing us to stand firm when life's storms come our way.

Spending time in Scripture strengthens our faith and aligns our hearts with God's will. The more we know and understand His Word, the more prepared we are to face challenges with resilience and clarity. Today, let's commit to making God's Word the foundation of our lives, allowing His truth to guide us, protect us, and equip us for every good work.

Prayer:
Dear Lord, thank You for the gift of Your Word, which provides strength, guidance, and wisdom. Help me to build my life on a solid foundation, rooted in Your truth. Open my heart to understand and apply Your teachings so that I may stand firm in faith and reflect Your love in everything I do. In Jesus' name, Amen.

Action Step:
Take a few minutes to read a passage of Scripture that speaks to your heart. Reflect on how it applies to your life and what God may be teaching you through it. Commit to making God's Word a daily part of your life, allowing it to build a strong foundation of faith.

Speak aloud: "Lord, I commit to building my life on the foundation of Your Word. Help me to hear, understand, and live by Your truth."

Journaling Prompt:
Reflect on the importance of having a strong foundation in God's Word. How does Scripture strengthen your faith and guide your actions? Write down any passages that resonate with you today, along with insights or thoughts on how you can apply them in your daily life.

As you journal, remember Psalm 119:105: *"Your word is a lamp to my feet and a light to my path."* Let this verse remind you that God's Word lights the way, guiding you through life's twists and turns with wisdom and clarity.

Reflection on the Journey Ahead:
Building a foundation in God's Word prepares us for life's challenges and helps us grow in wisdom and strength. As you continue this journey, let God's Word be your guide, protecting you and equipping you with all you need to walk faithfully. Trust that as you deepen your understanding of Scripture, you'll grow closer to God and stronger in your faith.

Day 25 Takeaway:

Today, you focused on building a foundation in God's Word, allowing His truth to be the rock upon which you stand. Remember that a life rooted in Scripture is resilient and equipped for every season. Let God's Word guide you daily, strengthening your faith and drawing you closer to Him.

DAY 26: EMBRACING GOD'S PEACE

Scripture Reading:
"Be anxious for nothing, but in everything by prayer and supplication, with thanksgiving, let your requests be made known to God; and the peace of God, which surpasses all understanding, will guard your hearts and minds through Christ Jesus." —Philippians 4:6-7 (NKJV)

Reflection:
Today, let's focus on embracing God's peace, especially in times of worry and uncertainty. Philippians 4:6-7 calls us to release our anxieties to God through prayer and thanksgiving, promising that His peace—greater than any human understanding—will protect our hearts and minds. Peace is a gift from God, one that calms our fears, strengthens our faith, and allows us to face life's challenges with a calm assurance.
When we cast our cares on God, we're choosing to trust in His love and power. God is fully capable of carrying our burdens and guiding us through any situation. Today, let's surrender our worries to Him, allowing His peace to fill our hearts and minds and draw us closer to His presence.

Prayer:
Dear Lord, thank You for offering Your peace that surpasses all understanding. I bring my worries and fears to You, asking that You replace them with Your calming presence. Help me to trust in Your love and to embrace the peace that comes from knowing You are in control. Thank You for guarding my heart and mind, keeping me secure in Your care. In Jesus' name, Amen.

Action Step:
Think of a specific worry or concern weighing on your heart. Take a few moments to release it to God in prayer, trusting that He will carry it for you. As you do, thank Him for His peace and remind yourself that He is with you every step of the way.

Speak aloud: "Lord, I release my worries to You, trusting in Your peace to fill my heart. Thank You for being my strength and my comfort."

Journaling Prompt:
Reflect on any anxieties or concerns that have been weighing on your mind. How does it feel to surrender these worries to God? How has God's peace helped you in times of trouble? Write down any thoughts or experiences as you trust in His presence and embrace His peace.

As you journal, remember 1 Peter 5:7: *"Casting all your care upon Him, for He cares for you."* Let this verse remind you that God cares deeply for you and is ready to carry your burdens, offering His peace in return.

Reflection on the Journey Ahead:
Embracing God's peace allows us to live with calm assurance, knowing that He is in control. As you continue this journey, make it a habit to surrender your worries to Him, allowing His peace to guard your heart and mind. Let His presence be a source of comfort and strength in every season.

Day 26 Takeaway:

Today, you focused on embracing God's peace, choosing to surrender your anxieties to Him. Remember that God's peace is a gift, calming your heart and strengthening your faith. Trust in His presence and let His peace fill every part of your life.

DAY 27: TRUSTING IN GOD'S TIMING

Scripture Reading:
"For I know the plans I have for you, says the Lord, plans for peace and not for evil, to give you a future and a hope." —Jeremiah 29:11 (NKJV)

Reflection:
Today, let's focus on trusting in God's timing. Jeremiah 29:11 reminds us that God's plans for us are good, filled with hope and a future. Though we often want things to happen on our schedule, God's timing is always perfect. When we trust Him, we can rest in the assurance that He sees the bigger picture and is working for our good, even in seasons of waiting.

Trusting in God's timing requires patience and faith. It's a reminder that God is faithful, that He is always at work, and that His plans are far greater than we could imagine. Today, let's release our desire to control the timing of our lives and choose to rest in His perfect plan.

Prayer:
Dear Lord, thank You for Your perfect timing. Help me to trust You, even when I don't understand or when I grow impatient. Teach me to rest in Your plans and to believe that Your timing is always for my good. Give me the faith and patience to wait on You, knowing that You are working for my future and hope. In Jesus' name, Amen.

Action Step:
Think of an area in your life where you're waiting on God's timing—whether it's a decision, a goal, or a dream. Surrender it to God today, asking for patience and faith to trust that His timing is perfect.

Speak aloud*:* "Lord, I trust Your timing and release my plans into Your hands. Help me to wait patiently, knowing that Your plans for me are good."

Journaling Prompt:
Reflect on how you feel about God's timing in your life. Are there areas where you struggle to let go of control or feel impatient? How can trusting in His timing bring peace to your heart? Write down any insights or reflections as you focus on His plans for you.

As you journal, remember Proverbs 3:5-6: *"Trust in the Lord with all your heart, and lean not on your own understanding; in all your ways acknowledge Him, and He shall direct your paths."* Let this remind you that God's timing and plans are trustworthy, leading you toward a future filled with hope.

Reflection on the Journey Ahead:
Trusting in God's timing frees us from anxiety, allowing us to rest in His care. As you continue this journey, choose to wait patiently on His timing, believing that He has good things in store. Each day, remind yourself that His plans are greater than you can imagine, and He is always working for your good.

Day 27 Takeaway:

Today, you focused on trusting in God's timing, choosing to surrender control and rest in His perfect plans. Remember that God's timing is always for your good, and let this trust bring you peace and hope as you wait on Him.

DAY 28: LIVING WITH PURPOSE

Scripture Reading:
"For we are His workmanship, created in Christ Jesus for good works, which God prepared beforehand that we should walk in them." —Ephesians 2:10 (NKJV)

Reflection:
Today, let's focus on living with purpose, recognizing that God has created each of us with unique gifts and a meaningful calling. Ephesians 2:10 reminds us that we are God's workmanship, carefully crafted to fulfill good works that He has prepared for us. Embracing this purpose means understanding that our lives have a significant role in God's greater plan, and that each day brings opportunities to make a positive impact.

Living with purpose doesn't require grand gestures; it's about walking faithfully in the small things, seeking to reflect God's love in every interaction and choice. Today, let's ask God to reveal more of His purpose for our lives, trusting that He will guide us in each step as we seek to honor Him with our unique gifts and passions.

Prayer:
Dear Lord, thank You for creating me with purpose and for preparing good works for me to walk in. Help me to live each day with intention, embracing the gifts You've given me. Show me how to use my life to serve and honor You. Guide my steps, and let my life reflect Your love and grace. In Jesus' name, Amen.

Action Step:
Think about one area of your life where you feel called to make an impact—whether through your work, relationships, or service. Ask God to guide you in this area and to help you walk with purpose, trusting that He has prepared you for this calling.

Speak aloud: "Lord, I choose to live with purpose, seeking to use my life to serve and honor You. Show me the path You have set for me and guide my steps each day."

Journaling Prompt:
Reflect on what it means to live with purpose. What are some unique gifts, talents, or passions God has given you? How might He be calling you to use them for His glory? Write down any thoughts, ideas, or insights as you seek to embrace the purpose God has for your life.

As you journal, remember Jeremiah 29:11: *"For I know the plans I have for you, says the Lord, plans for peace and not for evil, to give you a future and a hope."* Let this encourage you to trust that God's plans for you are good and that He has uniquely prepared you for His work.

Reflection on the Journey Ahead:
Living with purpose brings meaning and direction to our lives. As you continue this journey, seek God's guidance in using your gifts and talents for His glory, trusting that He has prepared good works for you. Each day, let His love and wisdom shape your actions, knowing that your life has a unique and beautiful purpose in His plan.

Day 28 Takeaway:

Today, you focused on living with purpose, embracing the unique calling God has placed on your life. Remember that you are His workmanship, created for good works that He has prepared for you. Let this purpose guide you as you continue to walk with Him, seeking to reflect His love and grace in all you do.

DAY 29: CULTIVATING A SPIRIT OF GENEROSITY

Scripture Reading:
"But this I say: He who sows sparingly will also reap sparingly, and he who sows bountifully will also reap bountifully. So let each one give as he purposes in his heart, not grudgingly or of necessity; for God loves a cheerful giver." —2 Corinthians 9:6-7 (NKJV)

Reflection:
Today, let's focus on cultivating a spirit of generosity. 2 Corinthians 9:6-7 reminds us that God loves a cheerful giver, and that generosity flows from the heart. When we give freely, we reflect God's own generosity toward us. Generosity isn't only about financial giving; it includes sharing our time, our attention, and our love with others, seeking to be a blessing wherever we go. A generous heart doesn't give out of obligation but out of love, seeking to reflect God's goodness to others. Today, let's look for opportunities to give joyfully, whether through small acts of kindness, a word of encouragement, or a helping hand. When we give with a joyful heart, we experience the blessing of being a vessel of God's love.

Prayer:
Dear Lord, thank You for Your boundless generosity toward me. Help me to reflect Your love through a generous heart. Teach me to give freely, without hesitation, and to seek ways to bless others. Let my generosity be an offering to You, filled with joy and love. In Jesus' name, Amen.

Action Step:
Choose one intentional act of generosity today, whether it's giving your time, a helping hand, or a resource to someone in need. Do it quietly and with joy, focusing on reflecting God's love rather than seeking recognition.

Speak aloud: "Lord, help me to give freely and joyfully, reflecting Your generous love to those around me."

Journaling Prompt:
Reflect on how it feels to give generously. How has generosity—whether given or received—impacted your life? Write down any thoughts or experiences, and consider how God may be calling you to cultivate a heart that gives freely and cheerfully.
As you journal, remember Proverbs 11:25: *"The generous soul will be made rich, and he who waters will also be watered himself."* Let this encourage you that as you give, God replenishes you, allowing you to continue being a blessing to others.

Reflection on the Journey Ahead:
Cultivating a spirit of generosity draws us closer to God, helping us to reflect His love in meaningful ways. As you continue this journey, let generosity become a natural part of who you are, trusting that God will fill your heart with joy and contentment as you give. Let every act of generosity be a quiet offering to God.

Day 29 Takeaway:

Today, you focused on cultivating a spirit of generosity, choosing to give with a joyful heart. Remember that generosity reflects God's own love, and that each act of kindness and giving brings you closer to His heart. Let this spirit of giving be part of your journey, blessing others and deepening your connection with God.

DAY 30: FINDING STRENGTH IN GOD DURING CHALLENGES

Scripture Reading:
"But those who wait on the Lord shall renew their strength; they shall mount up with wings like eagles, they shall run and not be weary, they shall walk and not faint." —Isaiah 40:31 (NKJV)

Reflection:
Today, let's focus on finding strength in God, especially during times of challenge. Isaiah 40:31 reminds us that when we wait on the Lord, He renews our strength. In life's struggles, we often feel weak and weary, but God promises to sustain us, lifting us up and giving us the resilience we need to persevere.

Leaning on God's strength means acknowledging our own limitations and trusting in His power. When we let go of self-reliance and allow Him to guide us, we find the courage to face challenges with a hopeful heart. Today, let's bring our burdens to God and trust that He will renew our strength, allowing us to walk forward with confidence and faith.

Prayer:
Dear Lord, thank You for being my source of strength. I come to You with my burdens, trusting that You will renew my spirit and carry me through. Help me to let go of my worries and lean on Your power. Teach me to wait on You, knowing that in Your presence, I find all the strength I need. In Jesus' name, Amen.

Action Step:
Identify a specific challenge you're facing right now. Take a few moments to release it to God in prayer, asking Him to strengthen you. As you go about your day, remind yourself that God is with you, guiding you and renewing your spirit.

Speak aloud: "Lord, I release my challenges to You, trusting that You will give me strength and carry me through. Thank You for being my refuge and my strength."

Journaling Prompt:
Reflect on a time when you felt strengthened by God during a difficult season. How did leaning on His power impact you? Write down any thoughts or memories, and thank Him for the times He has carried you. Consider how His strength can sustain you now as you face any current challenges.

As you journal, remember Psalm 46:1: *"God is our refuge and strength, a very present help in trouble."* Let this reassure you that God is always near, offering you strength and support whenever you need it.

Reflection on the Journey Ahead:
Finding strength in God allows us to face any challenge with peace and confidence. As you continue this journey, make it a habit to lean on Him in both trials and everyday moments. Trust that He is always with you, renewing your spirit and giving you the courage to move forward.

Day 30 Takeaway:

Today, you focused on finding strength in God, choosing to rely on His power during times of challenge. Remember that God is your refuge and strength, and He is always present to sustain you. Let His strength be your foundation as you continue to walk in faith.

DAY 31: SERVING OTHERS IN NEW WAYS

Scripture Reading:
"I was naked, and you clothed Me; I was sick and you visited Me; I was in prison and you came to Me." —Matthew 25:36 (NKJV)

Reflection:
Today, let's focus on exploring new ways to serve others, particularly those who may be isolated or in difficult circumstances. In Matthew 25:36, Jesus reminds us that when we serve the sick, the imprisoned, or the needy, we are truly serving Him. Sometimes, reaching out to others requires us to step beyond our usual routines, but these acts of service can be deeply impactful, both for the person being served and for us as we grow in compassion and humility.

Visiting the elderly, connecting with those in prison, or participating in a ministry that serves the marginalized are powerful ways to reflect God's love. These small acts of kindness remind people that they are valued and loved, not only by us but by God. Today, let's ask God to open our hearts and show us new ways to serve, trusting that each act of compassion is a way to honor Him.

Prayer:
Dear Lord, thank You for reminding me of the importance of serving those who may feel forgotten. Open my heart to new ways of showing Your love, whether through visiting the elderly, supporting those in prison, or simply being present for someone in need. Guide my steps and help me to serve with a humble and compassionate heart. In Jesus' name, Amen.

Action Step:
Consider a new way you might serve others, such as volunteering at a senior center, writing letters to someone in prison, or joining a ministry that serves those in difficult situations. Take a small step toward making this

commitment, trusting that God will use your service to bring hope to those in need.

Speak aloud: "Lord, I am open to new ways of serving others. Lead me to those who need to feel Your love and kindness, and help me to serve with a willing heart."

Journaling Prompt:
Reflect on the importance of serving others in ways that may be outside of your comfort zone. How might reaching out to the elderly, the imprisoned, or the marginalized impact your faith and growth? Write down any thoughts or feelings as you consider how God might be calling you to serve in new ways. As you journal, remember Hebrews 13:3: *"Remember the prisoners as if chained with them—those who are mistreated—since you yourselves are in the body also."* Let this verse remind you that we are all connected and that God calls us to extend compassion and solidarity to those in need.

Reflection on the Journey Ahead:
Serving others in new ways helps us grow in compassion and humility, drawing us closer to God's heart. As you continue this journey, remain open to the opportunities He places before you to make a difference in someone's life. Every act of kindness reflects His love and brings hope to those who need it most.

Day 31 Takeaway:

Today, you focused on serving others in new ways, choosing to step beyond your comfort zone to reflect God's love. Remember that each act of kindness brings hope to those who may feel forgotten, reminding them of God's presence. Let this spirit of compassion guide you as you continue to serve and grow in your faith.

DAY 32: SEEKING GOD'S WISDOM IN DECISIONS

Scripture Reading:
"If any of you lacks wisdom, let him ask of God, who gives to all liberally and without reproach, and it will be given to him." —James 1:5 (NKJV)

Reflection:
Today, let's focus on seeking God's wisdom in our decisions. James 1:5 encourages us to ask God for wisdom when we feel uncertain. His wisdom provides us with the insight to make choices that honor Him and bring peace to our lives. Whether the decision is big or small, seeking God's guidance helps us align our choices with His will.

When we approach decisions with prayer and a heart open to God's leading, we can trust that He will guide us. God's wisdom is perfect; it brings clarity, peace, and strength, allowing us to move forward confidently. Today, let's ask God for wisdom in our lives, trusting Him to illuminate the path before us.

Prayer:
Dear Lord, thank You for offering Your wisdom freely to those who ask. I bring my decisions to You today, seeking Your guidance and clarity. Teach me to listen for Your voice and to trust that You are directing my steps. Help me to make choices that honor You and reflect Your love and grace. In Jesus' name, Amen.

Action Step:
Think of a decision you're facing, whether big or small. Bring it to God in prayer, asking Him for wisdom and guidance. Take a moment to listen for His direction, trusting that He will provide clarity.

Speak aloud: "Lord, I seek Your wisdom in all my decisions. Guide me to choose paths that honor You and reflect Your will."

Journaling Prompt:
Reflect on a recent decision where you sought God's guidance. How did His wisdom shape the outcome? How can you make seeking His wisdom a regular part of your decision-making? Write down any thoughts or insights as you commit to bringing future choices before God.

As you journal, remember Proverbs 3:5-6: *"Trust in the Lord with all your heart, and lean not on your own understanding; in all your ways acknowledge Him, and He shall direct your paths."* Let this verse remind you to trust God's wisdom over your own, knowing that He will guide you in the right direction.

Reflection on the Journey Ahead:
Seeking God's wisdom helps us navigate life with peace and clarity. As you continue this journey, make it a habit to bring your decisions to Him, trusting that He will provide the insight you need. Let each choice be an opportunity to grow in faith, knowing that God's guidance will never lead you astray.

Day 32 Takeaway:

Today, you focused on seeking God's wisdom in your decisions. Remember that when you trust in His guidance, He will direct your paths with peace and clarity. Let this commitment to seeking His wisdom shape each choice you make, drawing you closer to Him.

DAY 33: THE POWER OF SUPPLICATION AND PRAYING FOR OTHERS

Scripture Reading:
"I urge, then, first of all, that petitions, prayers, intercession, and thanksgiving be made for all people." —1 Timothy 2:1 (NKJV)

Reflection:
Today, let's focus on the power of supplication—bringing the needs of others before God in prayer. In 1 Timothy 2:1, we are encouraged to lift up others in prayer, asking God to bless, heal, and guide them. Praying for others not only brings us closer to God, but it also deepens our empathy and compassion, helping us carry each other's burdens.

When we pray for others, we're reminded that God is at work in every life. Our prayers have the power to bring comfort, peace, and strength to those who may be struggling. Today, let's take time to lift up friends, family, and even strangers, entrusting them to God's care and trusting that He hears our prayers.

Prayer:
Dear Lord, thank You for the gift of prayer and the opportunity to lift others up to You. I bring before You the needs of those around me, asking for Your healing, guidance, and blessing in their lives. Help me to be faithful in prayer, showing love and compassion through my words. May my prayers be an offering that brings hope and comfort to others. In Jesus' name, Amen.

Action Step:
Choose three people to pray for today—perhaps a friend, family member, and someone in your community. Take time to pray specifically for their needs, asking God to bless and guide them. If you feel led, consider reaching out to let them know you're praying for them.
Speak aloud: "Lord, I lift up those around me to You. Strengthen them, comfort them, and let them feel Your presence."

Journaling Prompt:
Reflect on how praying for others impacts your heart and your relationship with God. How does interceding for others deepen your compassion and empathy? Write down any thoughts or feelings, and consider how you can make supplication a regular part of your prayer life.
As you journal, remember James 5:16: *"The effective, fervent prayer of a righteous man avails much."* Let this verse remind you that your prayers are powerful and meaningful, bringing encouragement and blessing to those for whom you pray.

Reflection on the Journey Ahead:
Praying for others allows us to show love in action, connecting us with God and our community. As you continue this journey, seek to make supplication a regular practice, lifting up the needs of those around you with faith and compassion. Trust that God hears every prayer and that He is at work in each life.

Day 33 Takeaway:

Today, you focused on the power of supplication, choosing to lift others up in prayer. Remember that praying for others is an act of love and faith, bringing comfort and hope to those in need. Let this practice of interceding for others strengthen your relationship with God and deepen your compassion

DAY 34: CULTIVATING A HEART OF GRATITUDE

Scripture Reading:
"In everything give thanks; for this is the will of God in Christ Jesus for you." —1 Thessalonians 5:18 (NKJV)

Reflection:
Today, let's focus on cultivating a heart of gratitude, choosing to give thanks in all circumstances. 1 Thessalonians 5:18 reminds us that it is God's will for us to be thankful, regardless of what life brings. Gratitude shifts our focus from what we lack to the many blessings around us, helping us recognize God's goodness and provision.

When we practice gratitude, we open our hearts to joy, peace, and contentment. Gratitude doesn't ignore life's challenges; rather, it helps us see them in light of God's presence and faithfulness. Today, let's commit to finding reasons to be thankful, trusting that even the smallest blessings are gifts from God.

Prayer:
Dear Lord, thank You for the countless blessings You pour into my life. Teach me to be grateful in all things, recognizing Your goodness and love in every season. Help me to see challenges as opportunities to grow and to praise You for the strength You provide. May my heart overflow with gratitude today and always. In Jesus' name, Amen.

Action Step:
Take a few moments to list five things you're grateful for today—big or small. As you reflect on each one, thank God for these blessings. Practice seeing His hand in all aspects of your life, and let gratitude fill your heart.
Speak aloud: "Lord, thank You for Your endless blessings. I choose to focus on Your goodness and to live with a heart of gratitude."

Journaling Prompt:
Reflect on the impact gratitude has had on your life. How does a thankful heart bring peace, joy, or clarity? Write down any thoughts or experiences as you commit to cultivating gratitude daily.
As you journal, remember Psalm 100:4: *"Enter into His gates with thanksgiving, and into His courts with praise. Be thankful to Him, and bless His name."* Let this remind you that gratitude brings you closer to God, opening your heart to His love and joy.

Reflection on the Journey Ahead:
A heart of gratitude transforms our outlook, bringing us closer to God and filling us with joy. As you continue this journey, seek to make thankfulness a daily practice. Trust that even in difficult seasons, God's blessings surround you, and His presence is a constant source of comfort.

Day 34 Takeaway:

Today, you focused on cultivating a heart of gratitude, choosing to see God's blessings in every part of your life. Remember that thankfulness opens the door to peace, joy, and contentment. Let gratitude become a habit, drawing you closer to God and filling your life with His grace.

DAY 35: THE IMPORTANCE OF STUDYING GOD'S WORD

Scripture Reading:
"Your word is a lamp to my feet and a light to my path." —Psalm 119:105 (NKJV)

Reflection:
Today, let's focus on the importance of studying God's Word, setting aside dedicated time to read, meditate, and understand Scripture. Psalm 119:105 reminds us that God's Word is our guide, lighting the way in both simple and challenging moments. Just as we need physical nourishment, our spirits are nourished by the truth, encouragement, and wisdom found in the Bible. Engaging deeply with Scripture brings clarity, builds resilience, and strengthens our connection to God. When we dedicate time to studying His Word, we open ourselves to the Holy Spirit's guidance, allowing God's truth to transform our hearts and minds. Today, let's commit to spending meaningful time in the Bible, trusting that His Word will provide the wisdom and peace we need.

Prayer:
Dear Lord, thank You for the gift of Your Word, which is my source of strength, guidance, and hope. Help me to approach Scripture with an open heart and a hunger to know You more. Teach me to prioritize time in Your Word, allowing Your truth to shape my thoughts and actions. Thank You for the wisdom and light that Your Word brings to my life. In Jesus' name, Amen.

Action Step:
Set aside 15-30 minutes today to study a passage of Scripture. Choose a verse or chapter that speaks to you and take time to read, reflect, and seek God's wisdom in its meaning. Consider taking notes or journaling what you learn as you allow God's Word to speak to your heart.

Speak aloud: "Lord, I dedicate this time to studying Your Word. Open my heart to understand and apply Your truth, guiding my steps and deepening my faith."

Journaling Prompt:
Reflect on how studying God's Word impacts your relationship with Him. How does Scripture provide strength, comfort, or wisdom in your life? Write down any insights or thoughts as you commit to making Bible study a regular part of your time with God.

As you journal, remember Joshua 1:8: *"This Book of the Law shall not depart from your mouth, but you shall meditate in it day and night, that you may observe to do according to all that is written in it. For then you will make your way prosperous, and then you will have good success."* Let this verse remind you that studying God's Word brings lasting guidance and blessing.

Reflection on the Journey Ahead:
Studying God's Word is essential to a life grounded in faith and wisdom. As you continue this journey, seek to make time in Scripture a priority, knowing that each verse brings you closer to God. Trust that He will reveal new truths and insights as you deepen your understanding of His Word.

Day 35 Takeaway:

Today, you focused on the importance of studying God's Word, choosing to dedicate time to understanding and applying Scripture. Remember that God's Word is a source of strength, guidance, and joy. Let regular Bible study be a vital part of your relationship with Him, providing light for your path.

DAY 36: DEVELOPING A HEART OF HUMILITY

Scripture Reading:
"Humble yourselves in the sight of the Lord, and He will lift you up." —James 4:10 (NKJV)

Reflection:
Today, let's focus on cultivating a heart of humility. James 4:10 reminds us that when we humble ourselves before God, He will lift us up. Humility helps us recognize that our strengths, wisdom, and blessings come from God, not from ourselves. A humble heart is one that is open to learning, ready to serve, and willing to depend on God for guidance and strength.

When we live with humility, we are better able to see others with compassion and put their needs above our own. Today, let's ask God to work in our hearts, helping us grow in humility so that we can honor Him in all we do and serve others selflessly.

Prayer:
Dear Lord, thank You for being my strength and source of wisdom. I come before You with a humble heart, acknowledging that all I have comes from You. Help me to live with humility, seeing others through Your eyes and serving with a selfless heart. May my life reflect Your grace and love. In Jesus' name, Amen.

Action Step:
Identify one area where you can practice humility today, such as putting someone else's needs first, offering encouragement, or simply listening without needing to be heard. Take this action with a heart focused on honoring God and serving others.

Speak aloud: "Lord, teach me to walk humbly with You, recognizing that my strength and wisdom come from You alone."

Journaling Prompt:
Reflect on what it means to live with a humble heart. How does humility impact your relationship with God and your ability to serve others? Write down any thoughts or experiences as you ask God to help you grow in humility.

As you journal, remember Philippians 2:3-4: *"Let nothing be done through selfish ambition or conceit, but in lowliness of mind let each esteem others better than himself. Let each of you look out not only for his own interests, but also for the interests of others."* Let this verse remind you that humility is not about thinking less of yourself, but about valuing others and relying on God's strength.

Reflection on the Journey Ahead:
A heart of humility allows us to grow closer to God and to serve others with grace and compassion. As you continue this journey, seek to live with a humble spirit, trusting that God will guide and lift you up. Let humility shape your faith, drawing you into a deeper relationship with Him.

Day 36 Takeaway:

Today, you focused on developing a heart of humility, recognizing God as the source of your strength and wisdom. Remember that humility draws you closer to God and allows you to serve others selflessly. Let humility be a foundation in your walk with Him.

DAY 37: WALKING IN THE SPIRIT

Scripture Reading:
"If we live in the Spirit, let us also walk in the Spirit." — Galatians 5:25 (NKJV)

Reflection:
Today, let's focus on walking in the Spirit—inviting the Holy Spirit to guide our daily steps, decisions, and actions. In Galatians 5:25, Paul encourages us to live in alignment with the Spirit, who gives us the power to overcome challenges and to reflect God's character. Walking in the Spirit means surrendering our own ways and allowing the Spirit to guide us in wisdom, patience, kindness, and love.
When we walk in the Spirit, our lives become a reflection of God's presence and love in the world. We no longer react solely based on human impulses or emotions; instead, we respond with patience, compassion, and wisdom that come from God. As we approach the end of this 40-day journey, let's commit to keeping in step with the Spirit, allowing Him to fill our lives with peace, joy, and purpose.

Prayer:
Dear Lord, thank You for the gift of Your Holy Spirit, who guides, comforts, and strengthens me. Help me to walk in Your Spirit each day, listening for Your voice and following Your lead. Fill my heart with Your love and wisdom so that my actions reflect Your presence within me. May my life be a testimony to Your grace, bringing hope and peace to those around me. In Jesus' name, Amen.

Action Step:
Reflect on one area in your life where you want to invite the Holy Spirit's guidance. Whether it's a relationship, a personal goal, or a specific challenge,

ask the Holy Spirit to direct your steps and give you clarity. Take time throughout the day to pause and listen for His promptings.

Speak aloud: "Dear Heavenly Father, You are the Lord of Lords and King of Kings, I invite You to lead me today. Guide my thoughts, my words, and my actions. Help me to walk in step with You, surrendering my ways to Your wisdom. I choose to follow You, trusting that You will direct my path and fill my heart with peace, joy, and love. Lord, may my life reflect Your presence and bring glory to Your name. Amen."

Journaling Prompt:
Consider how walking in the Spirit might change the way you approach your daily life. Are there specific areas where you struggle to surrender to His guidance? Write down any insights, prayers, or commitments to rely more fully on the Holy Spirit in your journey.

Reflection on the Journey Ahead: Walking in the Spirit isn't a destination—it's an ongoing journey that brings us closer to God each day. Let the Spirit's presence in your life lead you with wisdom and love, strengthening you in every season.

Day 37 Takeaway:

Today, you committed to walking in the Spirit, allowing God's presence to guide each step. Remember that the Holy Spirit is your constant Helper, bringing you peace, wisdom, and strength as you continue your walk with Him.

DAY 38: BEARING FRUIT IN EVERY SEASON

Scripture Reading:
"He is like a tree planted by streams of water that yields its fruit in its season, and its leaf does not wither. In all that he does, he prospers." — Psalm 1:3 (ESV)

Reflection:
God desires for us to bear fruit in every season, much like a tree planted by streams of water. In Psalm 1:3, we are reminded that when we root ourselves in God's Word and His presence, we are nourished and equipped to produce fruit—character, love, and good works—that brings Him glory. Bearing fruit doesn't mean life is always easy; instead, it signifies a heart that remains steady and flourishing despite circumstances. God provides everything we need to grow and thrive in Him.
Today, reflect on the importance of being spiritually grounded, so that your life can be a source of blessing and strength. Even in challenging times, your faith can remain firm and vibrant. As you seek Him, trust that He will use you to produce fruit that reflects His love, joy, peace, and patience. Allow Him to nourish you through His Word, fellowship with other believers, and time spent in prayer.

Prayer:
Father, thank You for planting me in Your love and truth. Help me to be rooted deeply in You so that my life may bear fruit in every season. Let Your Spirit fill me with Your joy, patience, and kindness, and guide me to be a blessing to others. In every situation, may I bring honor to Your name and reflect Your character. Amen.

Action Step:
Think about one "fruit of the Spirit" (Galatians 5:22-23) that you want to grow in this season. Whether it's love, joy, peace, patience, kindness, goodness, faithfulness, gentleness, or self-control, commit to nurturing this quality through prayer and intentional action.

Speak aloud: "Holy Spirit, I invite You to lead me today. Guide my thoughts, my words, and my actions. Help me to walk in step with You, surrendering my ways to Your wisdom. I choose to follow You, trusting that You will direct my path and fill my heart with peace, joy, and love. Let the fruits of the Spirit—love, joy, peace, patience, kindness, goodness, faithfulness, gentleness, and self-control—grow within me and flow through me to bless others. Lord, may my life reflect Your presence and bring glory to Your name. Amen."

Journaling Prompt:
Write about a time in your life when you felt spiritually nourished and rooted in God. How did this grounding help you bear fruit? Consider areas where you might need deeper roots or more consistent spiritual practices to thrive.

Reflection on Growth: Just like a tree, growth in our spiritual life often happens beneath the surface before it's visible to others. Stay connected to God, and trust that He is working in you even in unseen ways.

Day 38 Takeaway:
Today, you committed to bearing fruit by staying rooted in God's presence. Remember, each season brings unique growth and fruitfulness. Embrace God's work in you, and trust that your life will flourish and bless others as you remain planted in Him

DAY 39: STRENGTHENED IN WEAKNESS

Scripture Reading:
"But he said to me, 'My grace is sufficient for you, for my power is made perfect in weakness.' Therefore I will boast all the more gladly of my weaknesses, so that the power of Christ may rest upon me." — 2 Corinthians 12:9 (ESV)

Reflection:
Sometimes, we may feel as though our weaknesses disqualify us or make us less useful to God. Yet, the opposite is true. When we acknowledge our weaknesses and surrender them to God, we create space for His strength to shine through us. Our limitations become opportunities for His power to be displayed in ways that bring Him glory and draw others to Him.

Today, reflect on the areas in your life where you feel weakest. Rather than hiding or avoiding them, consider how God might want to work through those very places. His grace covers every shortfall, every insecurity, and every fear. Let His promise reassure you that His strength is perfected when you are most aware of your need for Him. Trust that He can use you powerfully, even in those areas where you feel least capable.

Prayer:
Lord, thank You for reminding me that Your grace is enough, especially in my weakness. Help me to see my limitations not as hindrances but as opportunities for Your power to be displayed. Teach me to lean on You fully and to trust that You will equip me for everything You call me to do. In my weakness, be my strength. Amen.

Action Step:
Identify an area of weakness in your life and invite God to work through it today. It might be something like a relationship challenge, a difficult task, or an area where you feel inadequate. Ask God to show His strength through you, and be open to His guidance as you move forward.

Speak aloud: "Lord, I thank You that Your grace is sufficient for me. In my weaknesses, Your strength is made perfect, and I choose to trust in Your power rather than my own abilities and understanding. I surrender my insecurities, my fears, and my limitations to You, knowing that You can use even the weakest parts of me to bring glory to Your name. May Your power rest upon me and shine through me, reminding others of Your love and faithfulness. In every moment of weakness, I will boast in Your strength. Amen."

Journaling Prompt:
Write about a time when you felt weak, but God's strength carried you through. How did that experience help you understand His grace and power in a new way? Reflect on what it means for you to trust God with your weaknesses and let His strength shine through them.

Reflection on Surrender: Remember that God does not expect us to be perfect but to be available. He delights in using imperfect vessels to display His perfect strength and love.

Day 39 Takeaway:

Today, you embraced your weaknesses as a place where God's power can shine. Trust in His grace, knowing that He is strong where you are not. Let Him work through every limitation, and watch how His strength transforms your life and touches those around you.

DAY 40: A HEART OF WORSHIP

Scripture Reading:
"Come, let us bow down in worship, let us kneel before the Lord our Maker; for he is our God and we are the people of his pasture, the flock under his care." — Psalm 95:6-7 (NIV)

Reflection:
Worship is more than singing songs or attending services; it's an ongoing response to God's love and faithfulness. True worship flows from recognizing who God is and embracing His greatness, goodness, and grace. When we set our hearts on Him, we're reminded of our purpose and our dependence on His strength.

In worship, we're invited to draw a close, surrendering all that we are to a God who cares for us like a shepherd with his flock. Worship reminds us that we are not alone—we are guided, protected, and loved by the One who made us. In these moments of worship, our spirits are refreshed, and we find ourselves restored in His presence.

Today, allow worship to be your response to God's goodness. Take time to acknowledge Him as the source of every blessing in your life. Whether you're singing, praying, or simply pausing to reflect, let your heart overflow with gratitude and praise. Let God's presence fill you with peace and strength as you dwell in worship.

Prayer:
Father, I come before You with a heart of gratitude and worship. Thank You for being my Creator, my Shepherd, and my source of life. Help me to live in a constant state of worship, always aware of Your presence and love. Teach me to honor You with my thoughts, words, and actions, and to find my true rest and joy in You. In Jesus' name, Amen.

Action Step:
Find a quiet moment today to enter into personal worship. Whether through a worship song, a walk in nature, or time in prayer, allow yourself to focus completely on God, expressing your gratitude and love for Him. Reflect on how He has been your guide and protector.

Speak aloud: "Lord, I bow before You in worship and rejoicing in Your name, recognizing that You are my Creator, my Shepherd, and the source of every blessing in my life. I thank You, Lord, for difficult times and long-suffering, for in these moments I am reminded that I must decrease so that You may increase. Please soften and humble my heart so that I may fully surrender my heart, my thoughts, and my actions to You in praise. Teach me to live and walk each day in Your Spirit and in worship, honoring You in everything I do. Thank You for Your faithfulness, Your protection, and Your love. Let my life be a reflection of Your greatness and goodness. I praise You, Lord, and I find my rest and joy in Your presence. Amen."

Journaling Prompt:
What does worship mean to you? How can you bring a heart of worship into your daily life? Write about times when worship has helped you feel closer to God or has given you peace. Consider how you can cultivate a spirit of worship in the ordinary moments of your day.

Reflection on Worship: Worship is a response to God's love and a declaration of His worth in our lives. It refocuses our hearts and minds on what truly matters and invites God's presence to be our source of strength.

Day 40 Takeaway:

Today, you focused on worship as a way of life, bringing your heart to God with gratitude and praise. Remember that worship is an invitation to draw close to God, allowing His presence to renew and strengthen you daily. May you carry this heart of worship into every day ahead.

CLOSING REFLECTION: A JOURNEY OF INTENTIONAL GIVING AND CLOSENESS TO GOD

As we reach the end of this devotional journey, my prayer is that these days have deepened your relationship with God and enriched your understanding of what it means to live a life of intentional giving. Through this process, I hope you've come to see the tithe not merely as a monetary gift but as a reflection of our dedication—a portion of our "first fruits" offered daily to our Creator. This kind of giving, whether in time, talents, energy, or love, invites us into a lifestyle of surrender and gratitude.

Being intentional in our offerings to God means recognizing His presence in every part of our lives. Just as we give the first of our resources, let's also give Him our first thoughts, our best efforts, and our full hearts. In every area, God invites us to honor Him by giving back a piece of what He has so freely given us. As we do, we invite His blessings, His peace, and His wisdom into every corner of our lives.

Thank you for taking this journey. May the insights you've gained and the habits you've cultivated guide you in drawing closer to God each day. May you continue to grow in faith, walking with the assurance that God is with you, providing, guiding, and loving you every step of the way.

Final Prayer:
Father, thank You for this journey, for the wisdom You've imparted, and for drawing us closer to You. Help us to live with hearts full of gratitude and generosity, remembering to offer You the first and best of all we have. Let our lives be a testimony of Your goodness and faithfulness, and may our actions reflect a heart that truly desires to honor You. In Jesus' name, Amen.

Thank you for the opportunity to walk through this with you, and may your journey ahead be richly blessed as you continue to live a life of intentional devotion and giving.

ABOUT THE AUTHOR

Anthony "Mark" Gray lives in Willow Spring, North Carolina, with his beloved wife, Paula. Together, they have raised two wonderful sons, Andy and Zach Gray, who are now grown. Mark serves as an Elder at Friendly Chapel Church in Benson, North Carolina, where he is dedicated to sharing God's Word and encouraging others in their walk with Christ.

Mark has a deep love for the Lord and cherishes the precious gift of life. Walking with Jesus daily brings him joy and purpose, and he considers it an honor to share his faith through this devotional. Having experienced God's rescuing grace firsthand, Mark reflects often on how his Shepherd, Jesus Christ, sought out and saved him when he was lost.

With a heart full of gratitude and devotion, Mark hopes this devotional inspires others to draw closer to God, trust in His unfailing love, and embrace the abundant life found in walking with Him.

Printed in Great Britain
by Amazon